Strategic Ch ||||||||||||||||||
T0265236
in Science and
Technology

Korea in the Era of a Rising China

Somi Seong, Steven W. Popper

Prepared for the
Korea Institute of Science and Technology Evaluation and Planning

 CENTER FOR ASIA PACIFIC POLICY

This research was prepared for the Korea Institute of Science and Technology Evaluation and Planning.

Library of Congress Cataloging-in-Publication Data is available for this publication.

ISBN 0-8330-3746-3

Published 2005 by the RAND Corporation
1776 Main Street, P.O. Box 2138, Santa Monica, CA 90407-2138
1200 South Hayes Street, Arlington, VA 22202-5050
201 North Craig Street, Suite 202, Pittsburgh, PA 15213-1516
RAND URL: http://www.rand.org/
To order RAND documents or to obtain additional information, contact
Distribution Services: Telephone: (310) 451-7002;
Fax: (310) 451-6915; Email: order@rand.org

Preface

Active investment in China, finding more market opportunities in China, and strengthening the cooperative relationship with China have so far been successful paths for Korean companies and the government to take in response to China's new economic might. However, it is not certain whether Korea can maintain its market position in both Chinese and world markets in the future because China is becoming more competitive in many industries where Korea currently has a relative advantage. What should Korea do to maintain its economic dynamism in light of these uncertainties? What would be appropriate strategies and policies for Korea to pursue, particularly in science and technology?

This report identifies Korea's main economic concerns related to China's rapid industrial development and growing science and technology (S&T) capabilities, presents alternative S&T strategies for Korea to follow, and shows how those strategies could affect Korea's economic prosperity. The report should interest science and technology policymakers in Korea and other governments who are concerned with the opportunities and challenges of a rising China. It is expected to serve as a good reference work for the debates that are prevalent in Korea, and its methodology will be of general interest to Korea's policy analysis community.

This research was sponsored by the Korea Institute of Science and Technology Evaluation and Planning (KISTEP). It was conducted under the auspices of the RAND Corporation's Center for Asia-Pacific Policy (CAPP), which aims to improve public policy by providing decisionmakers and the public with rigorous, objective research on critical policy issues affecting Asia and U.S.-Asia relations. The Center for Asia Pacific Policy is part of International Programs at RAND, which conducts research for a wide range of U.S. and international clients, including governments, foundations, and corporations.

For more information on the Center for Asia Pacific Policy, contact the director, Nina Hachigian. She can be reached by email at Nina_Hachigian@rand.org; by phone at 310-393-0411, extension 6030; or by mail at RAND, 1776 Main Street, Santa Monica, California 90407-2138. More information about RAND is available at www.rand.org.

Contents

Figures

Tables

Summary

China—Opportunity or Threat?

China has become the biggest recipient of foreign direct investment in the world. It is the largest trading country in Northeast Asia, surpassing even Japan, and a major export market for many Asian economies including Korea, Japan, and Taiwan. As China's economy becomes more powerful, many see it as presenting a formidable threat as well as an opportunity. Koreans are no exception in having these mixed feelings toward China. Even if we confine our interest to the economic arena, Korea's list of potential threats from China is considerable: the hollowing out of the manufacturing sector, job loss, and loss of shares of the world market and the China market.

The effect of China's economic rise on the Korean economy has been significant. China is now Korea's largest trading partner and the largest destination for Korea's foreign direct investment. As Korea's economic relationship with China continues to develop, economic threats and shocks emanating from China could be as significant as China's positive effects on Korean economy.

Active investment in China, finding more market opportunities in China, and strengthening the cooperative relationship with China have so far been desirable paths for Korean companies and governments to take. However, what should Korea do to ensure the prosperity of its economy and to better face uncertainty in the future?

What would be appropriate strategies and policies for Korea to pursue, particularly in science and technology (S&T)?

In this context, the Korea Ministry of Science and Technology (KMOST) asked RAND through the Korea Institute of Science and Technology Evaluation and Planning (KISTEP) to assess the benefits and risks of Korea's economic engagement with China and to draw policy implications for Korea, focusing in particular on the science and technology progress of both countries.

Objective, Approach, and Structure of the Study

This study identifies Korea's main economic concerns related to China's rapid industrial development and growing S&T capabilities. Its aim is to show alternative S&T strategies that Korea may follow and how those strategies may affect Korea's economic prosperity.

Using trade, investment, and research and development (R&D) data, we analyze the general economic relationship between Korea and China at the industry as well as the aggregate level to uncover general trends and the macro configuration of the technological capabilities of both countries. Next, we analyze the main drivers of change in China's S&T progress, compared with those of Korea, in the framework of China's national innovation system. Micro-level analyses of China's institutional arrangements, the relative strengths of its R&D performers—industry, university, and research institutes—and its national strategies and programs complement the macro-level analysis.

Based on both macro data analysis and micro-level examination of institutional structure and resource allocation, we develop a simple model of the Korean economy and alternative S&T strategies that Korea could follow. We then show how those strategies affect Korean prosperity, explicitly considering the uncertainties that Korea will confront. The model captures key elements of our concern, such as the technology gap between the two countries, international competitiveness, and such external shocks as a possible change in China's macroeconomic performance. In our future scenario, we introduce an approach that minimizes the maximum "regret" associated with pursuit of one or another of the strategies. *Regret* is defined as the difference between the result of a chosen strategy in a specified state of the world and the result that would have been obtained if the optimal strategy for those circumstances had been pursued.

Korea's Main Economic Concerns About a Rising China

So far, Korea has enjoyed the opportunities provided by China's growing markets. Korea's major export products to China are intermediate goods, such as core components and equipment, and Korea's exports have grown along with China's economy and exports. However, it is uncertain whether this positive relationship between Korea and China can be sustained in the long run.

Even though equipment and components comprise Korea's major export items to China, Korea does not have a comparative advantage in those items. Korea actually imports core components and high-tech equipments from Japan and other industrialized countries. In fact, this has been the main source of Korea's trade deficit with Japan, which is larger than its deficit with its other trading partners. Industrialized countries such as the United States and Japan are the dominant players in production of core components and equipment.

While Korea has found a niche in the Chinese market in terms of price competitiveness, this niche may be harder to maintain as competition in the Chinese component and equipment market increases. A combination of advanced technologies from the world's leading companies and China's cheap and disciplined labor may create new markets in China and remove Korea from the market niche it now enjoys.

The competitive pressure from China may have been relatively weak since the 1990s because the world economy has been booming with a strong U.S. economy and the explosive growth of China. But in the event of a worldwide recession—because of an economic downturn in China, high oil prices, or other reasons—the once-positive relationship between Korea and China could easily become negative. In addition, whether China can successfully slow down its overheated economy and sustain its potential growth path is still a matter of controversy.

What would be an appropriate strategy for Korea to pursue to maintain its economic dynamism in light of these uncertainties? Is Korea moving in the right direction to ensure a prosperous future? Among many factors, answers to these questions will depend on whether Korea can maintain its technological leadership, at least in selected areas of products and technologies.

S&T Indicators and Trends

In Terms of Aggregate S&T Capability Indices, Korea Is Ahead of China

The Technological Achievement Index (TAI) of the United Nations Development Programme (UNDP), the ArCo Index, and RAND's Science and Technological Capacity Index (STCI) all show that Korea's aggregate S&T capacity is higher than that of China. According to STCI, Korea is in the second-tier group and ranks 18th out of 76 countries (see Table 3.1 in Chapter Three). According to the TAI and ArCo index, Korea is in the top group in S&T capability and ranks 5th and 19th out of 72 and 172 countries, respectively, while China is to the third group and ranks 45th and 85th, respectively.

The rankings on the aggregate S&T capacity indices, however, must be interpreted carefully. Many individual indicators used in constructing the aggregate capacity indices were standardized by size of population or GDP. Therefore, China's lower ranking on the TAI, ArCo, and STCI indices, in comparison with Korea's, does not necessarily mean that China's absolute S&T capability or potential is inferior to Korea's.

China Is Ahead of Korea in Absolute Scale of R&D Investment and Human Resources

While Korea's R&D intensity is more than twice as high as that of China, the absolute level of China's R&D expenditure of China is 10 percent higher than that of Korea. If purchasing power parity (PPP) is used as a measure, China's R&D expenditure is three times as great as that of Korea. The number of scientists and engineers per 10,000 population in Korea is 2.5 times that of China, whereas the absolute number of full-time equivalent scientists and engineers of China is seven times that of Korea. China's large and increasing number of S&T personnel gives it an obvious advantage in human resources. China currently ranks second in the world in number of R&D personnel. It has more doctoral degree holders than Japan, and the number of Chinese who have completed higher education in the S&T field is close to that of the United States. China's full-time equivalent R&D personnel was over 1 million in 2002, second only to that of the United States and roughly six times that of Korea.

China Has a Strong Research Capability in Basic Science

Investment in basic research is often used as a proxy for future-oriented research activities and long-term innovation capabilities. In China, less than 6 percent of total R&D funding is allocated to basic research, which amounts to half of Korea's basic research investment. However, China publishes twice as many scientific papers as Korea does.

According to the world ranking of ISI Essential Science Indicators covering the ten-year period between 1993 and 2003, China ranked 9th and Korea ranked 16th, based on the number of scientific papers in all fields catalogued by the Science Citation Index (SCI). In terms of total number of citations, China ranked 19th whereas Korea was not in the top 20 during the period. China's rate of research paper publication is also rising much faster than Korea's. Although some say that a majority of China's researchers are not yet world-class thinkers and that Chinese R&D results are not as influential as those of the world's leading researchers, China has made consistent and rapid progress in recent years—not just in the quantity but also in the quality of papers published.

Why does China's scientific paper publication outperform its investment in basic research? One of the reasons is that China has abundant human resources for R&D in universities and research institutes—resources that can be tapped for marginal or sometimes no extra funding. Graduate students often serve as low-cost researchers, and there were more than 500,000 graduate students enrolled in China in 2002—nearly twice as many as in Korea. Another reason may lie in the difference in accumulated knowledge stock in basic science. Like other socialist countries, China has emphasized the importance of "big sciences" such as aerospace, nuclear science, oceanography, and other basic sciences; even now, this tradition continues to some extent in the context of national security.

Patent Data Show That China Has Limited Invention Capabilities

The number of patent applications in China and U.S. patent awards to Chinese nationals suggests that China is still a country with relatively low capabilities in invention and innovation. In 2002, Chinese citizens accounted for only 19.4 percent of invention-type patents in China. In 2003, China's share of foreign patent applications in the United States was only 0.1 percent. In contrast, Japan's was 43.8 percent, Taiwan's was 6.5 percent, and Korea's was 4.9 percent.

Another salient feature is that the industrial sector is not the major player in invention-type patents in China. Chinese universities, research institutes, and government together held twice as many valid invention-type patents as industry at the end of 2001. This contrasts sharply with foreign patenting activities in China, where the lion's share of valid invention patents are owned by enterprises.

The Technology Review's (TR's) Annual Patent Scorecard ranks the U.S. patent portfolios of 150 top technology companies in eight industries including aerospace, computers, electronics, semiconductors, telecommunications, biotechnology and pharmaceuticals, chemicals, and automotive. These data provide not only the patent counts for each company but also other indices based on frequency of citation of the patents and links to scientific research. No Chinese company was listed on the TR Patent Scorecard as of 2003, whereas twelve Korean companies are listed.

Of course, patents statistics are only one of several indicators of innovation capability. Technology assimilation capability and the linkage of technology to the global R&D network may be as important as invention capability in China since its economy is still in the development stage.

China's National Innovation System and R&D Strategies

To understand China's S&T capabilities and its future potential, we must understand its underlying and stated national goals and objectives. China's S&T capabilities are built on and enhanced by national strategies, policies, and plans. These are implemented by means of complex institutional arrangements and various R&D projects, augmented by the development of S&T human resources and boosted by foreign direct investment (FDI) inflows and outflows, as well as international cooperation and exchange.

S&T and Education Are the Two Pillars of Economic Development in China; Openness Is a Major Strategy

In 2002, the Chinese government set an ambitious long-term goal to quadruple its GDP to US $4 trillion with a per capita GDP of $3,000 by the year 2020. The government plans to achieve this goal by "taking a new road to industrialization by implementing the strategy of rejuvenating the nation through science and education and that of sustainable development."

Jiang Zhemin's Report to the 16th CPC Party Congress in 2002 set out the guidelines for implementing the strategy of "rejuvenating the nation through science and education." It also emphasized that economic development was not to be isolated but should be increasingly open to the outside world in order to "actively participate in international economic and technological cooperation as well as competition."

From the strategy and the guidelines, we clearly observe that openness is important to China and that S&T progress and education are the two main pillars of its future economic prosperity.

Universities Are Major Knowledge Creators in China

Universities are the major players in Chinese research—not only basic science but also applied research and commercialization. In 2002, universities accounted for 77 percent of Chinese science and engineering papers in international publications.

Universities in China also provide a strong R&D base for applied research and commercialization. By the end of 2002, 105 National Key Laboratories (i.e., more than two-thirds of the total key labs), 43 National Engineering Centers, 22 science and technology parks, and six technology transfer centers were affiliated with Chinese universities.

Beijing University and Tsinghua University are especially prominent in breeding high-tech spin-offs. Qinghua Tongfang and Beijing University's Founder's Group are good examples of spin-offs. These companies have grown big enough to leave the universities. But although they are listed on stock exchanges and have their own headquarters, the universities are still their main shareholders.

On the other hand, the fact that China's major R&D capability is concentrated in sectors other than industry may slow down growth in innovation capability. This is because industry responds to market incentives more effectively than do universities and government research institutes.

China's Indigenous Industrial Sector Is a Relatively Weak Link in Its National Innovation System

Industry is the main innovator in most Organization of Economic Cooperation and Development (OECD) countries including Korea. In China, however, universities and government research institutes and laboratories are the main R&D performers. China's industrial sector in general has yet to improve its innovation capability to the point of becoming a leader in the country or the world.

The Chinese industrial sector depends heavily on foreign technology sources. Almost 90 percent of China's high-tech exports consist of processed goods that use imported or foreign-supplied materials. Considering China's record-breaking economic growth, it was probably a better strategy for Chinese companies to adopt readily available technologies instead of innovating on their own, which takes much more time than purchasing the technologies. A similar phenomenon was observed in Korea at an earlier stage of its development.

Of course, there are many prominent high-tech companies in China. However, compared with global technology leaders, they are still small and weak in the areas of sales and intellectual property rights. For example, Huawei is an exemplary high-tech company that has achieved great success in global marketing and technological progress. It attracted global attention when it was involved in an intellectual property rights dispute with Cisco Systems, the world's largest maker of routers and switches that transmit data and direct Internet traffic. However, Huawei's R&D expenditure in 2003 was only 13 percent of that of Korea's Samsung Electronics. Huawei's total sales amounted to about 11 percent of Samsung's in the same year.

Many large-scale state-owned companies in China are listed among *Fortune* magazine's global top 500 companies. However, they are basically in traditional industries, such as banking, insurance, energy, manufacturing, and utilities.

Interaction with the Foreign Sector Has Contributed Significantly to China's Economic and Technological Progress

Foreign direct investment in China has contributed significantly to its rapid economic development. An International Monetary Fund (IMF) study showed that FDI in China has contributed nearly 3 percent to China's annual GDP growth during the 1990s. In other words, FDI explains almost a third of China's GDP growth rate while its share of total fixed asset investment averaged only 12.5 percent between 1993 and 2002.

By the end of 2002, the number of employees in foreign-invested enterprises (FIEs) had reached 23.5 million, accounting for 11 percent of China's urban workforce. FIEs have conducted extensive training of Chinese employees to enable them to use the advanced technologies supplied by the FIEs and to operate within their advanced management systems. In 2002, FIEs accounted for 33.4

percent of China's industrial output, 52.2 percent of its total export, and 21 percent of its tax revenue.

Interaction with the foreign sector has contributed significantly to the rise of high-tech industries in China. Chinese electronics and telecommunication equipment manufacturers, such as Huawei, Zhongxing, TCL, and Haier, are good examples of how the massive inflow of FDI has enabled Chinese indigenous companies to become serious competitors with incumbent foreign firms. Huawei, for instance, started out selling foreign-made telecom switches and then became a globally competitive producer of switches and routers.

Evaluation of China's NIS and Strategic Direction

China's strategic strength lies mainly in its openness as an engine of growth, its strong bargaining power due to its huge domestic market, and its abundance of highly educated people. China's vulnerability lies in the fact that its major R&D capability is concentrated in sectors other than industry, which may slow down innovation.

This weakness is in part inherited from China's tradition of government-led technology push in S&T development during the era of the Cold War and the communist economic system. Because of this very weakness in "demand pull" factors due to its relatively weak industrial R&D capability, the Chinese government again has tended to entrust most of the national R&D programs to R&D institutes and universities. However, this strategy may risk further weakening the link between R&D bodies and market incentives as well as the innovation capability of China's industrial enterprises.

It may take a considerable time for China's national innovation system to become as efficient as those of advanced countries.

China's enormous and fast-growing domestic market is a great asset that can leverage the nation's economic development and S&T progress. Because of this huge market, China has been able to attract more FDI and more multinational corporation (MNC) R&D centers, bargain for more technology transfer, produce abundant high-quality scientists and engineers, and even pursue its own technology standard.

Not only manufacturing but also R&D activities are attracted to China's large market and abundant human resources. According to a survey by *The Economist* magazine, China has become the top destination for overseas R&D by multinational corporations, despite its poor protection of intellectual property rights. Some studies already assert that China is not only the manufacturing powerhouse of the world but also a research powerhouse. China is making rapid progress in S&T, with a solid conceptual framework, a focused strategy, and a favorable infrastructure and economic environment.

Options for Korea

The limited size of Korea's domestic market, always one of its weaknesses, has driven Korea to pursue an export-oriented development strategy. With the rise of China, however, Korea's outward-looking strategy, which is based on selling manufactured commodities to the world, may be less effective than before. Unless Korean companies sell goods with better technological content and higher value-added than Chinese companies, Chinese companies will be in a better position to produce most manufactured goods.

What can Korea do to ensure its prosperity in the future? Korea does not have the depth of knowledge in basic science or generic technologies that Japan and the United States have. It is relatively capable in applied technology and commercialization, but this relative strength might not be sustainable as a long-term advantage because applied technologies and commercialization capability are more easily obtained than basic and generic technologies. Especially in China, progress in applied technology and commercialization could be much more rapid than in other developing countries because of such positive drivers as huge FDI, significant training and education by FIEs, and the establishment of R&D centers by MNCs.

Support R&D Intensity but Obtain R&D Efficiency Too

High R&D intensity is one of Korea's strengths. However, Korea has a longstanding problem with relatively low R&D efficiency. Several factors may contribute to this. As we will see in Chapter Three, although Korea is one of the most capable countries in terms of R&D-to-GDP ratio, the density of scientists and engineers in Korea is not as high as in other countries.

To support its intensive R&D activities, Korea will need more high-quality scientists and engineers. This, of course, cannot be achieved in the medium term. To correct this weakness, Korea must build networks with others in the "global brain pool."

Another major determinant of R&D efficiency is the level of existing knowledge stock. If the knowledge stock is low, R&D investment flows do not produce as much as in countries with a high knowledge stock. R&D investment is a necessary condition to increase the knowledge stock itself. In other words, to reach a certain level of R&D efficiency, Korea must accumulate knowledge stock, and this in turn will need R&D investment.

Should Korea Be More Engaged in the China Market?
Korea has the option to complement its weaknesses by tapping into China's strengths. Abundant human resources for both production and R&D and a large and a fast-growing domestic market are China's most salient strengths—strengths that Korea does not have. Such strategies as inducing foreign investors in China to source from Korea or finding complementary markets with China have been widely discussed in the existing literature in Korea.

In fact, Korea has been heading in this direction already by investing in China, producing in China, and conducting R&D in China. Proximity to China is another factor that has strengthened the economic relationship between Korea and China. As long as their economic environments are in harmony and the mutually beneficial economic relationship between the two countries is sustained, this would be a good bet for Korea. However, we are not sure what the net effect of greater engagement with China will be in the future.

Will Korea continue to enjoy opportunity in China? Could there be a "boomerang effect" from China? Could China carve out a portion of the world market and exclude Korea? There are no straightforward answers to these questions, which are part of Korea's conflicting perceptions about China.

Education for Creative and Innovative Thinking

Creative and innovative thinking is more than merely absorbing existing knowledge. Fostering true creativity will require educational reform at all levels—primary, secondary, and tertiary. First, Korea will need an adequate supply of highly educated and trained researchers to make further progress in S&T. As of 2003, the ratio of scientists and engineers to the total higher education degree holders in Korea was significantly higher than in the United States, Japan, and many other industrialized countries. However, the number of scientists and engineers per 10,000 people is lower in Korea than in other advanced countries, mainly because the general ratio of highly educated people to the total population is lower in Korea. Therefore, Korea must continue to support broader access to higher education. In addition, the quality of graduate-level education needs more attention. Compared to that of advanced countries, graduate-level education in Korea is quite underdeveloped, even though it has been improving recently. The Korean Ministry of Education and Human Resource Development has put a great deal of effort into its "BK 21" project to improve graduate education in the 21st century.

Labor unions in Korea are known to be highly confrontational. Developing a well-educated, versatile workforce that is able to conduct R&D and convert it to innovation could serve as a win-win solution to the current confrontational relationship between business and labor. Such an educational strategy could connect the knowledge-intensive industrial activities of the demand side with the more expensive (relative to China) but highly skilled labor force from the supply side. Ideally, Korea might want to aim for a society in which its citizens are paid as much as those with similar education and skills in advanced countries, instead of targeting a specific level of per capita income. To achieve this goal, however, both business and labor need to be more innovative so that Korea's labor productivity will be as high as that in advanced countries.

Openness May Have to Be Korea's Strategy No Less Than China's
With "openness" as a growth engine, China has achieved explosive economic growth and impressive technological progress even though it is still a socialist country with a less sophisticated market system than some other developing countries. Few countries remain economically isolated since China opened its doors and other former socialist countries also made the transition to a market economy. However, in the eyes of foreign investors, Korea is still a hostile country for foreign investment. Many foreign business leaders think Korea is relatively isolated from active global networking.

Korea has not yet carved out a significant market in the internet or software business. In contrast, India takes over $100 billion in business from global software outsourcing by 185 Fortune 500 companies, according to the UNDP (2001). Both India and China have strong links with Silicon Valley, and the further development of information technology will continue to enhance the ability of multinational corporations to tie together globally distributed laboratories and firms.

Korea is a small country with a limited domestic market and is less attractive to foreign investors than China, Hong Kong, or Singapore. Therefore, Korea must emphasize both looking outward to explore opportunities on the world market and bringing in investment and business activities from abroad. Korea needs to pursue a strategy of allowing capital and labor to go abroad to find the best investment and job opportunities while at the same time improving the attractiveness of the country as a place for an increasingly mobile workforce to live.

Future Scenarios

Our simple model of the Korean economy emphasizes the importance of exports to China, the accumulations of assets generated by R&D, the narrowing of the technological differential between Korea and China, and changes in the size and nature of the Korean labor force.

In our analysis, we posit four strategic choices for Korean national planners. Although the strategies have names like "Base," "Openness," "R&D," or "Education," all should be considered mixed strategies made up of varying policy elements. Although these names evoke actions being discussed in Korean policy circles today, they are by no means to be considered definitive representations either of these policy alternatives or of the potential outcomes. The strategies are shown in Table S.1.

The analysis is conducted iteratively, seeking to assess the vulnerabilities of the candidate strategies to the uncertainties that have been identified, both parametric and structural. Our method allows us to view the performance of the strategies across large ensembles of alternative future scenarios. Using the metric of average annual rate of growth in GDP per capita for South Korea during the period leading to 2015, we assess each strategy across the ensemble of future scenarios.

Table S.1
Alternative Strategies for the Korean Economy

		Strategy		
Effect	Base	Openness; Refocus Attention Away from China	Focus on R&D	Focus on Education
Knowledge base growth rate	10%	10%	**13%**	10%
Capital investment rate	27%	**29.7%**	27%	27%
Commit to exporting to China	1.0	**0.6**	**0.8**	**0.8**
Job creation rate	0.01%	0.01%	0.01%	**0.02%**
Speed of narrowing the technology gap between Korea and China	−0.05%	−0.05%	**−0.03%**	−0.05%
Adjusted labor effect	1.0	**1.02**	1.0	**1.03**

NOTE: Input values that differ from those of the base case are shown in boldface.

For example, under normal conditions, the "Base" strategy would be better than the other three. But if there is prolonged stagnation in Chinese growth, the Base strategy would be overtaken by the performance of both the Education and Openness strategies. This illustrates how changes in assumptions may lead to radical shifts in policy recommendations when focusing on optimality as a criterion. In this sense, the analysis begins where more traditional analyses would conclude.

The analysis then proceeds to examine how each strategy would perform relative to the strategy that would be optimal for the set of circumstances that defines the scenario. This measure of "regret" for pursuing a chosen strategic course shifts the focus from optimization for any particular assumed most likely set of circumstances to the property of robustness. We find that the R&D strategy, while it may not be optimal in all scenarios, appears to be the strongest of the four candidate strategies when measured according to the criterion of robustness.

Maintaining a technical advantage over China—or at least keeping the technological gap between Korea and China as wide as possible—could be an insurance policy against stressful times in the future and could maintain the relative attractiveness of Korean products if there is a downturn in China's economic development. It would also give Korea a greater opportunity to explore and develop a presence in more-challenging markets.

Our four strategies are necessarily simple. Nevertheless, exploring the strategies highlights the value of their most important elements and serves as a means to make concrete some of the qualitative issues that are being discussed in Korea.

Acknowledgments

The authors would like to acknowledge the valuable insights and supports contributed by the following individuals and organizations:

Bruce Don and Charles Wolf offered exceedingly useful and insightful formal reviews that did much to improve our manuscript. Enlightening discussions with colleagues at RAND including Robert Anderson, Edward Balkovich, Gene Gritton, Nina Hachigian, William Overholt, Stephen Rattien, Caroline Wagner, Mark Wang, Anny Wong, and Feng Zeng helped the authors to polish their ideas. Miriam Polon skillfully edited the manuscript. Ze Cong and Arindam Dutta provided efficient research assistance, and Linda Lee and Stephanie Thompson offered well-organized administrative support.

The authors would like to express their thanks to Kungang Zheng, an outside consultant and an expert on China, for his inputs to Chapter Four. The authors are also thankful for informative and useful conversations with a number of people outside RAND: Young-il Park, Deputy Minister of Planning and Management, Korea Ministry of Science and Technology (KMOST); Hee-Yol Yoo, President, Korea Institute of Science and Technology Evaluation and Planning (KISTEP); Jiayu Cheng and Gong Zhong, National Research Center for Science and Technology Development (NRCSTD) of the China Ministry of Science and Technology; Harry Shum, Managing Director, Microsoft Research Asia in Beijing; Tong Wang, President, Samsung Telecom Research Center in Beijing; Lily Wu, Coventive Corporation; David Li, Tsinghua University; Pyung-sup Yang, Korea Trade Research Institute; Seong Bum Hong, Korea Science and

Technology Policy Institute (STEPI); Yeon-joon Cho, Korea Institute for International Economic Policy (KIEP); and many others who engaged in discussions with the authors in the course of this research.

Finally, the authors are grateful to KISTEP and KMOST for their financial support. Additional support for the model of the Korean economy and the scenario analysis, cornerstones of Chapter Six, was provided from RAND internal research funds, and thanks are due to Susan Everingham and Rachel Swanger, who encouraged us to apply for this funding.

Abbreviations

ArCo	Index of Science and Technology Policy Research at the University of Sussex (SPRU)
AT	aerospace technology
BT	biotechnology
CAE	Chinese Academy of Engineering
CAGR	compounded average annual growth rate
CAS	Chinese Academy of Sciences
CDMA	Code Division Multiple Access
CMOE	China Ministry of Education
CMOST	China Ministry of Science and Technology
CSIPO	China State Intellectual Property Office
CT	cultural technology
DRAM	Dynamic random access memory
EEHEIs	enterprises established by higher education institutions
EI	Engineering Index
ESI	export similarity index
ET	environmental technology
EVD	enhanced versatile disk
FDI	foreign direct investment
FIE	foreign invested enterprise

FTEs	full-time equivalents
GDP	gross national product
GERD	gross expenditure on R&D
GNI	gross national income
HR	human resources
HTIDZs	High Technology Industry Development Zones
ICs	integrated circuits
IMF	International Monetary Fund
IPOs	initial public offerings
IPR	intellectual property rights
IFS	International Financial Statistics (IMF)
ISTP	Index to Scientific and Technical Proceedings
ISO	International Organization for Standardization
IT	information technology
ITU	International Telecommunication Union
KDB	Korean Development Bank
KDI	Korea Development Institute
KIEP	Korean Institute for International Economic Policy
KIP	Knowledge Innovation Program
KISTEP	Korea Institute of Science and Technology
KITA	Korea International Trade Association
KMOE	Korea Ministry of Education and Human Resource Development
KMOST	Korea Ministry of Science and Technology
LCDs	Liquid crystal displays
MII	Ministry of Information Industry (China)
MLDP	Medium- to Long-Term Development Plan (China)
MNC	multinational corporation

MOCIE	Ministry of Commerce, Industry, and Energy (Korea)
NBS	National Bureau of Statistics (China)
NECs	National Engineering Centers (China)
NIS	national innovation system
NKLs	National Key Laboratories (China)
NRCSTD	National Research Center of Science and Technology for Development (China)
NSFC	National Natural Science Foundation of China
NT	nanotechnology
OECD	Organization of Economic Cooperation and Development
PCT	Patent Cooperation Treaty
PPCs	Productivity Promotion Centers (China)
PPP	purchasing power parity
QC	quality control
R&D	research and development
RCA	revealed comparative advantage
S&T	science and technology
SCI	Science Citation Index
SIPO	State Intellectual Property Office (China)
SITC	Standard International Trade Classification
SMEs	Small- and Medium-Sized Enterprises
SoC	System on a Chip
STCI	Science and Technological Capacity Index (RAND)
STEPI	Science and Technology Policy Institute (Korea)
STI	Science, Technology, and Industry (OECD)
SZHTP	Shanghai Zhangjiang High Tech Park
TAI	Technological Achievement Index (UNDP)

THTF	Tsinghua Tongfang Co. Ltd.
TR	Technology Review
UNCTAD	United Nations Conference on Trade and Development
UNDP	United Nations Development Programme
WAPI	Wired Authentication and Privacy Infrastructure
WEF	World Economic Forum
Wi-fi	Wireless fidelity, used generically when referring of any type of 802.11 network
WTO	World Trade Organization

CHAPTER ONE

Introduction

China's economy has grown at a phenomenal rate in the past two decades, providing new and vast market opportunities for Korea[1] as well as other countries.[2] China has become the biggest recipient of foreign direct investment in the world, the largest trading country in Northeast Asia—surpassing Japan—and a major export market for many Asian countries including Korea, Japan, and Taiwan. Beyond its economic performance, China also has played an increasingly important role in world politics including its central role in the Six-Party Talks to solve the problem of North Korea's nuclear program.

As China becomes more powerful both economically and diplomatically, many see it as presenting a formidable threat as well as an opportunity. Koreans are no exception to this mixed feeling toward China. Even if we confine our interest to the economic arena, Korea's list of potential threats from China is considerable: the hollowing out of the manufacturing sector; job loss; loss of shares of the world market and the China market; and competition from China in technology and commercialization.[3]

---

[1] We refer to South Korea in this report simply as "Korea."

[2] China's average annual growth rate since 1980 has been over 9 percent. Such sustained economic growth is rare in large economies. China's impressive economic development since its reform in 1979 is often compared to the emergence of the Japanese economy after the Meiji Restoration or to the U.S. economy at the beginning of the early twentieth century.

[3] China's rise as a political and military power is not the main focus of this study. We discuss only aspects of its economic rise.

The impact of China's economic rise on the Korean economy has been significant. Korea's exports to China grew more than 13-fold between 1992 and 2003, and China became the largest export destination for Korea in 2003, accounting for 18.1 percent of the country's total exports. China's importance as the destination for Korean exports surpassed that of the United States, its largest trading partner during the past 30 years.[4] Korean companies and individuals have also joined the investment rush into China to explore the business opportunities in a country growing at breakneck speed and to utilize the abundant and relatively cheap, yet disciplined, labor force for manufacturing. In 2002, Korea was the third-largest investor in China, after Hong Kong and Japan. In 2003, over 40 percent of Korea's foreign direct investment (FDI) went to China, making China the largest destination for Korea's FDI.[5]

As Korea's economic relationship with China continues to develop, the possible threats and shocks emanating from China could become as significant for the Korean economy as the positive effects of the relationship. Therefore, it is crucial for Korea to understand the opportunities and challenges that China's economic rise provide. In this context, the Korea Ministry of Science and Technology (KMOST) asked the RAND Corporation, through the Korea Institute of Science and Technology Evaluation and Planning (KISTEP), to assess the benefits and risks involved in Korea's economic engagement with China and to draw policy implications for Korea, with particular focus on the science and technology progress of both countries.

---

[4] In terms of total trade, the United States was still Korea's largest trading partner as of 2003. However, in the first eight months of 2004, China overtook the United States to become Korea's largest trading partner ($50.5 billion) and the largest source of Korea's trade surplus ($13.8 billion).

[5] Korea invested $2.5 billion, or 46.2 percent of its total overseas investment of $5.5 billion, in China.

Objective of the Study

The objective of the study is to analyze the relative strengths and vulnerabilities of Korea's current and future science and technology (S&T) capabilities—especially in relation to China's growing economic strength and S&T capabilities—and to assess their implications for Korea's S&T policy over the next ten years.

We attempt to answer the following questions: What factors and strategies would enable Korea to maintain its economic dynamism while increasing its activities in China? What role should the government play in technology advancement, compared with that of the private sector, for Korea to maintain a leading edge in selected areas of technological and R&D capability?

Approach

Using trade, investment, and research and development (R&D) data, we analyze the general economic relationship between Korea and China at the industry as well as the aggregate level to uncover general trends and the macro configuration of the technological capabilities of both countries. Next, we analyze the main drivers of change in China's S&T progress compared with those of Korea in the framework of the national innovation system.[6] Micro-level analysis of institutional arrangements, relative strengths of each R&D performer such as industry, university, and research institutes, and national strategies and programs will complement the macro analysis.

Based on the data analysis and micro-level qualifications, we develop a simple model of the Korean economy and alternative S&T strategies that Korea could follow. Then we show how those strategies may affect Korean prosperity, explicitly considering the many uncertainties that Korea will confront in the future. In our analysis of

---

[6] *The national innovation system* (NIS) consists of the network and interaction among different actors in the areas of knowledge creation, diffusion, and utilization. Refer to Freeman (1987), Metcalfe (1995), and IDRC (1997) for different sets of NIS definitions.

future scenarios, we introduce an approach to minimize the maximum regret associated with pursuit of one or another of the strategies—that is, how each strategy would perform relative to the strategy
that would be optimal for the set of circumstances that defines the
scenario.

Scope of the Analysis

Our analysis focuses mainly on a comparison between Korea and
China. We often introduce Japan as a third country in the comparison because it is needed to peg the other end of the scale against
which Korea is being gauged.[7] Especially when we analyze the economic capabilities of Korea and China, we assume a world with at
least three countries including Japan and often introduce the United
States and the rest of the world in addition.

As the configuration of technological leadership among Japan,
Korea, and China changes, the economic relationship among these
countries will also change. This study, however, does not cover how
Japan's economic and technological performance influences Korea's
options. We leave full-blown analysis of the three-country interactions as a topic for future research.

Outline of the Report

In the next chapter, we define Korea's main economic concerns about
China's rapid industrial development and growing S&T capabilities
and examine the validity of those concerns based on the evidence. We
look at how Korea's concerns are related to its own science and technology capability and strategies and highlight aspects of competition

---

[7] In terms of economic development, Korea is regarded as ahead of China but behind Japan.
Korea has been trying to catch up with Japan while remaining wary of being overtaken by
China.

and cooperation between Korea and China. We derive implications about the two countries' relative technological capabilities and trends.

In Chapter Three, we evaluate the current S&T capabilities of Korea and China in terms of quantitative measures and statistics. We address several questions: How is Korea's S&T potential evaluated in aggregate country-level S&T capability indices? How does it differ from China's? What are the main contributors to Korea's S&T capability? What are the relative weaknesses and strengths of each country as reflected by major S&T indicators? We compare the major trends in China's S&T activities with those of Korea and other countries to understand how those trends will influence China's future S&T progress.

Chapter Four analyzes factors that will change China's science and technology capability in the future. Using the theoretical framework of China's national innovation system, we explore the main drivers of rapid economic growth and science and technology progress. Our exploration consists of a micro-level analysis of the structure and motivation of China's national innovation system. We explain how different R&D performers, institutional arrangements, factor and product markets, and government R&D programs interact with each other and influence the pace and path of S&T progress in China. Finally, we put China's national innovation system together with its national economic goals and strategies and the contribution of the foreign sector.

In Chapter Five, we examine where Korea and China have positioned themselves in the race for technology progress, how S&T progress in the two countries will be oriented in the future, and what Korea's options are for making the best of its opportunities in the face of future challenges. We put together the analytical results in the previous chapters, ideas gleaned from the literature, and our understanding of Korea and China to suggest a collection of options from which Korea could choose. We focus on the micro characteristics of each strategy and the relevance of each strategy as an option for Korea.

In Chapter Six, we group the options suggested in the previous chapter into four broader strategies: a "Base" strategy, an "Openness" strategy, an "R&D-focused" strategy, and an "Education-focused" strategy. Using the metric of average annual rate of growth in GDP per capita for Korea during the period leading to 2015, we show how the payoff for each strategy changes across large ensembles of alternative future states. Our model explicitly considers changes in technological competitiveness, price competitiveness, and external shocks such as a change in China's macroeconomic performance.

Chapter Seven summarizes the results and concludes the report.

CHAPTER TWO

Korea's Main Economic Concerns About a Rising China

Although they are enjoying new market opportunities in China, Korean policymakers and industrial experts are worried about the threat from China. Korea's extensive economic engagement with China could very well make the old saying come true: A sneeze in China means flu in Korea. Even if we confine the discussion to the economic arena only, the list of potential threats encompasses the hollowing out of Korea's manufacturing sector, loss of jobs and market niche in China because of China's increased manufacturing capabilities, and an unpredictable market environment caused by competition with world-class companies operating in China. There is also concern about the Chinese economy overheating and the shockwaves that would be felt if China's bubble burst or the country went into an abrupt recession. Indeed, the sponsor of our study was also motivated, in part, by the above concerns.

In this chapter, we analyze the threats that a rising China might present to examine whether they are supported by evidence and how they are related to Korea's S&T capability and strategies.

Are China and Korea Competitive or Complementary?

Korea has been enjoying the opportunities presented by China's growing market. Korea's share of China's total imports increased from 1.1 percent in 1990 to 10.5 percent in 2002. As China rapidly expanded its share of the world market, Korea also improved its world export position. As Figure 2.1 shows, Korea's share in the world export market improved from 2.03 percent in 1991 to 2.53 percent in 2002, while China rapidly improved its share from 2.03 percent to 5.08 percent during the same period.

So far, Korea and China have been complementary rather than competitive in the area of trade. As Table 2.1 shows, Korea's major export products to China are components and other intermediate goods, whereas China's export to Korea are characterized by electronics products, textiles, and agricultural and mineral products. According to the Korea International Trade Association, 69.4 percent of Korea's export to China consisted of materials, components, and equipment in 2002. While China is exporting final goods to major markets, Korea is exporting intermediate goods to China and in this way actually exports indirectly to the industrialized world.

Figure 2.1
World Export Market Shares of Korea, China, Japan, and the United States

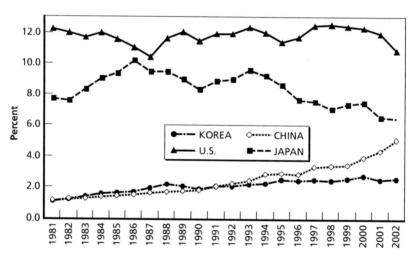

NOTE: Market shares are calculated using IMF's International Financial Statistics (IFS) trade data.
RAND *MG320-2.1*

Table 2. 1
Trade Between Korea and China, 2003 (US $millions)

Exports to China			Imports from China		
Total Exports	35,110	100%	Total imports	19,383	100%
Petrochemical products	6,784	19.32%	Agricultural and seafood	2,860	14.76%
Computers	3,687	10.50%	Computer and communications equipment	2,772	14.30%
Electronic components[a]	3,602	10.26%	Electronic components[a]	2,565	13.23%
General machinery	3,531	10.06%	Textile products	2,168	11.19%
Wireless communications equipment	3,115	8.87%	Mineral products	2,125	10.96%
Steel products	2,973	8.47%	Chemical products	1,803	9.30%
Petroleum products	1,717	4.89%	Steel products	1,082	5.58%
Fabrics	1,634	4.65%			

SOURCE: KITA database, "Trade and FDI Statistics," Korea Ministry of Commerce, Industry, Energy (MOCIE), www.mocie.go.kr/upload/statistics/total_statistical_list.asp?mode=2, accessed 23 November 2004.

[a] Electronic components include semiconductors.

Can the Mutually Beneficial Korea-China Trade Relationship Be Sustained in the Long Run?

The answer is not certain. For example, even though Korea's major export items to China are equipment and components, Korea does not have a comparative advantage in those items. The revealed comparative advantage (RCA) index of Korea's general industrial machinery and that of electric parts were 0.47 and 0.82 respectively as of 2000.[1]

In fact, Korea imports core components and high-tech equipment from Japan and other industrialized countries, and this has been the main source of Korea's trade deficit with Japan, which is larger than its deficit with its other trading partners. Industrialized countries such as the United States and Japan are the dominant players in the production of core components and equipment (Table 2.2).

Korea's weakness in parts and components is captured by the World Bank's RCA index of component production as reflected in the 2001 export statistics. Korea has an RCA in only nine component product groups out of 60.[2] The World Bank statistics do not indicate the technological contents of each component. However, quantitatively, Korea is far behind others. The United States has 40, Japan has 34, and China has 12 component product groups whose RCAs exceed unity. Component product groups with RCA exceeding unity for Korea includes steam boilers (6.68), electrothermic appliances (3.27), telecommunications equipment (2.70), outboard motors, not elsewhere specified (nes) (1.95), electric power machinery (1.94), electronic components, nes (1.58), textile machinery, nes (1.58), foundry equipment (1.32), and office and adding machinery (1.18). Korea has a revealed comparative advantage in 15.0 percent of the 60 parts and component products. This is even lower than the average percentage for other East Asian countries, which had 17.8 percent

---

[1] These data were obtained from KDI (2003). The RCA index of country i for product j is measured by the product's share of the country's exports in relation to the product's share of world total exports:

$$RCA_{ij} = \frac{(X_{ij} / X_{it})}{(X_{wj} / X_{wt})}$$

where w is the world and t means total. If the RCA index for country i's product j exceeds 1, that country is said to have a revealed comparative advantage in the product. Similarly, if the value is less than 1, the country has a revealed comparative disadvantage in the product.

[2] World Bank, http://lnweb18.worldbank.org/eap/eap.nsf/Attachments/Revealed+Comp.+Advantage7/$File/Revealed+Comparative+Advantage+7.pdf.

Table 2.2
Percentage of Parts and Component Products in Which East Asian Countries
Have a Comparative Advantage

Country	Exports—Production Operations (% of products with RCAs >1)			Imports—Assembly Operations (% of products with RCAs >1)		
	1985	1995	2001	1985	1995	2001
East Asia						
Brunei	–	3.3	0.0	0.0	18.3	23.3
Cambodia	–	1.7	0.0	0.0	15.0	11.7
China	6.7	11.7	20.0	41.7	55.0	53.3
Hong Kong	18.3	23.3	23.3	36.7	23.3	31.7
Indonesia	0.0	5.0	10.0	65.0	55.0	63.3
Japan	43.3	58.3	56.7	3.3	8.3	21.7
Korea	6.7	13.33	15.0	25.0	41.7	33.3
Lao PDR	–	0.0	0.0	–	11.7	11.7
Malaysia	8.3	15.0	18.3	53.3	45.0	43.3
Mongolia	–	0.0	0.0	–	21.7	11.7
Philippines	6.7	10.0	10.0	38.3	50.0	31.7
Singapore	20.0	23.3	20.0	36.7	40.0	38.3
Taiwan, China	20.0	31.7	28.3	13.3	35.0	31.7
Thailand	8.3	11.7	15.0	33.3	55.0	58.3
Vietnam	–	8.3	5.0	–	30.0	38.3
Average	13.8	20.3	21.7	34.7	40.8	40.7
Average excluding Japan	10.5	16.1	17.8	38.1	44.4	42.7
Comparison Countries						
Mexico	–	20.0	33.3	45.0	46.7	53.3
Hungary	10.0	31.7	25.0	71.7	53.5	46.7
Poland	–	30.0	41.7	51.7	48.3	61.7
United States	61.7	63.3	66.7	30.0	33.3	31.7

SOURCE: World Bank http://lnweb18.worldbank.org/eap/eap.nsf/Attachments/
Revealed+Comp.+Advantage1/$File/Revealed+Comparative+Advantage+1.pdf.
Comparison country statistics from Ng and Yeats (1999).

NOTE: Percentages based on 60 parts and component products.

(excluding Japan). Out of 60 parts and component products in the World Bank study, the United States, Japan, and China have RCAs larger than unity of 66.7 percent, 56.7 percent, and 20.0 percent respectively.[3]

Note that the above statistics do not consider the technological contents of the components that each country is exporting. Therefore, Korean equipment and component companies may have a comparative advantage in only a small number of components but may still be more profitable than Chinese companies.

This is one of the limitations of trade data. Trade statistics do not tell us about the level of value-added of the exports or the profitability of the trade. Our analysis of technological capability and company-level competence in the following chapters will complement this limitation.

Will Korea and China Be Increasingly Competitive in the Near Future?

If the past is any indication, competition between Korea and China will increase in the future. For example, Korea, China, and Japan all have an RCA in the information technology (IT) equipment industry[4] (see Figure 2.2), and it is also the largest export industry for all three countries (Table 2.3).

Korea's world market share of IT equipment increased from 3.6 percent in 1995 to 5.9 percent in 2000 (Figure 2.3). During the same period, China's market share has almost doubled from 3.5 percent to 6.6 percent. Japan's market share in world IT equipment export has

---

[3] World Bank, http://lnweb18.worldbank.org/eap/eap.nsf/Attachments/Revealed+Comp.+Advantage1/$File/Revealed+Comparative+Advantage+1.pdf.

[4] The IT equipment industry comprises products such as computers and office equipment, wireless and wired communication devices; broadcasting equipment; and TV, VTR, and other sound and picture facilities. It does not include semiconductors, electric and electronic parts, and other consumer electronic goods.

Figure 2.2
Comparison of RCA Indices for IT Equipment Industry: Korea, China, and Japan

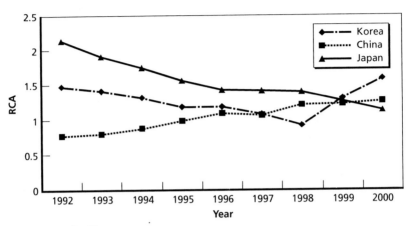

SOURCE: KDI (2003).
RAND *MG320-2.2*

been declining rapidly but still at 11.4 percent as of 2000, which is almost as high as the sum of Korea and China's market shares. For Japan, both RCA and export market share indicate that Japanese companies are less dominant in IT equipment export market than before. This might reflect not only the restructuring of the IT industry in Japan but also the increased overseas production by Japanese companies.[5]

The export similarity index (ESI) is often used in studies of international trade as a proxy to measure the extent of rivalry of two countries in the export market.[6] As Figure 2.4 shows, Korea's ESI

---

[5] According to Motohashi (2004), who cited statistics from Japan's Ministry of Finance, the cumulative amount of Japanese foreign direct investment in East Asia between fiscal years 1990 and 2001 was about 6 billion yen, 27 percent of which was in electronics.

[6] The ESI of countries a and b, where j is an industry product group, is defined as the summation over product groups of the minimum value of country a's share in a specific world product market and country b's share in the same market:

Table 2.3
Comparison of Export Structure: Korea, China, and Japan, 2000

Industry	Korea	China	Japan
Total Manufacturing	100.0	100.0	100.0
IT equipment	20.0	16.0	14.2
Semiconductors	12.4	1.9	8.4
Textile and garments	12.0	28.4	1.7
Chemicals	10.8	8.1	11.0
Automobile	9.0	1.7	17.7
Petroleum products	5.5	1.4	0.3
Industrial machinery	5.4	4.3	16.4
Vessels and other transportation	5.4	2.0	4.1
Electric and electronic parts	5.3	7.8	9.9
Metals	5.1	3.2	4.4
Manufactures of metals	2.0	3.6	1.6
Other manufacturing	1.6	9.8	1.6
Food and beverage	1.5	4.5	0.5
Consumer electronics	1.4	1.7	0.2
Paper products and printing	1.3	0.8	0.7
Precision machinery	1.1	3.0	6.2
Nonmetal mineral	0.6	1.8	1.1

SOURCE: KDI (2003).
NOTE: Figures may not sum to 100 because of rounding.

$$\mathrm{ESI}_{a,b} = \sum_{j=1}^{n} \min\left(\frac{X_{aj}}{X_{wj}}, \frac{X_{bj}}{X_{wj}}\right).$$

The same index can also be calculated over different geographic markets instead of the world market. The ESI is subject to aggregation bias and hence embodies a certain arbitrariness due to product choice. As the data are more finely disaggregated, the index tends to fall.

Figure 2.3
Comparison of Market Share in World Exports of IT Equipment: Korea, China, and Japan

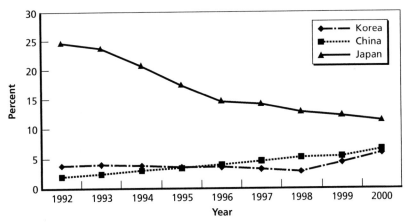

SOURCE: KDI (2003).
RAND MG320-2.3

Figure 2.4
ESI: Korea's Rivalry with China and Japan in the IT Equipment Industry

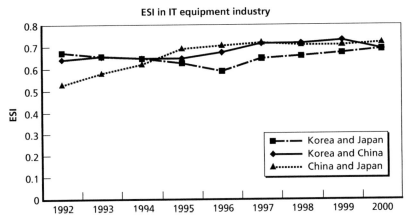

SOURCE: KDI (2003).
NOTES: The ESI varies between 0 and 1, with 0 indicating complete dissimilarity and 1 indicating identical export composition. The ESI was calculated at the Standard International Trade Classification (SITC) 4-digit level and aggregated into the IT equipment industry product group .
RAND MG320-2.4

with China and with Japan increased in the IT equipment industry, reflecting that Korea has caught up with Japan while China is gaining on both Korea and Japan.

Of course, indicators based on trade data should be interpreted carefully because of their inherent limitations. For instance, there is usually an aggregation bias. At the aggregated level, the export structures of different countries looks more similar than they really are. If we look at more disaggregated product levels, each country's targeted products or customer groups might be quite different. Thus, even though Korea, China, and Japan are all specialized in the production of IT equipment, the spectrum of IT products produced by each country and their technological content might be quite different, and their export products could be complementary rather than competitive.

However, a company or a country often expands its product portfolio into the same product groups or industry as another because of technological closeness or similar demand characteristics. Therefore, the industry-level analysis is useful for seeing the economic relationship among countries.

Other than the IT industry, rivalry between Korea and China is also expected in a number of areas—automobiles, petrochemicals, iron and steel, and shipbuilding—on whose development China has placed strategic emphasis. Since these products are major export products of Korea to China, Korea is under pressure either to move to the higher end of the market or to create a new product market with innovative new products.

Was Korea Squeezed Out of Markets in Industrialized Countries While Gaining Market Share in China?

Since 1996, Korea's major export destination has changed from the industrialized countries to the developing countries. Did Korea lose its share of other major markets, such as the United States and Japan, while it expanded its share in China and other developing countries? In the import markets of the United States and Japan, where China's penetration was rapid and high, Korea lost significant market share for ten years between 1988 and 1998. Korea's share of the U.S. import market decreased from 4.6 percent in 1988 to 2.6 percent in 1997, and its share of the Japanese market dropped from 6.3 percent to 4.7 percent during the same period. Part of this trend can also be observed by comparing Figures 2.5 and 2.6.

For a decade before the economic crisis of 1997, Korea was often described as being in a "nutcracker" between advanced countries such as Japan and developing countries in Southeast Asia. That is, Korea was under pressure from both developing countries and industrialized countries in the area of so-called international competitiveness—a melting-pot term for technological capability, production capability, commercialization, and marketing capabilities. On the trade side, this meant that Korea had been losing shares to developing countries on the low-end product market but had not successfully penetrated the high-end market where industrialized countries

Figure 2.5
Korea's Market Share by Regional Market

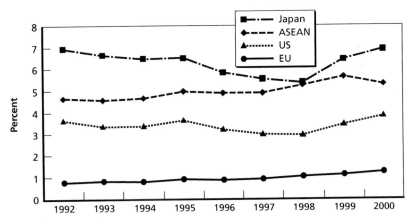

SOURCE: KDI (2003).
RAND MG320-2.5

Figure 2.6
China's Market Share by Regional Market

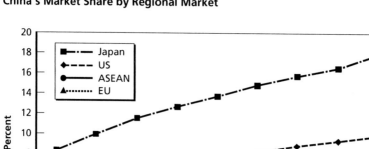

SOURCE: KDI (2003).
RAND MG320-2.6

operate. In fact, the profitability of Korean companies declined between 1989 and 1997.[7]

After 1998, Korea recovered its share of the U.S. and Japanese import markets. High growth in automobile and IT equipment exports contributed to Korea's recovery in the U.S. import market (Figure 2.7). Automobile and wireless telecommunication equipment accounted for 24.6 percent and 15.8 percent, respectively, of Korea's exports to the United States in 2003.[8] In the Japanese import market, petroleum products and IT equipment played a major role in Korea's recovery of market share, as we see from Figure 2.8.

The strong recovery after the economic crisis might reflect strengthened capability of Korean companies after the restructuring necessitated by the crisis and diligent R&D capacity-building since

---

[7] The profitability of publicly traded Korean companies was consistently below the cost of capital in 1989–1997, except for 1995. See Seong (2003).

[8] KITA database.

Figure 2.7
Korea's Share of the U.S. Import Market

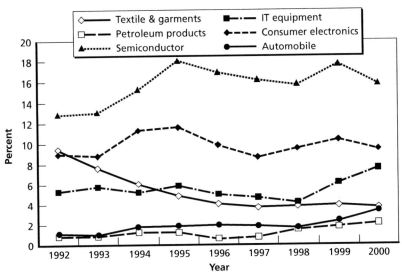

SOURCE: KDI (2003).
RAND MG320-2.7

the 1980s. At the same time, it could have been partly from the depreciated Korean won after the crisis and a favorable external economic environment, with the booming U.S. IT industry and the explosive growth of the China market. The favorable economic environment may be concealing structural vulnerabilities that Korea has not yet cured. Some Koreans think the nutcracker situation may again prevail in the near future unless Korean companies keep upgrading into high value-added products. Maintaining a market position in industrialized countries is desirable for Korean companies because the exposure to customers with relatively sophisticated demands enhances competitiveness (see Porter 1990). In this regard, Korea's export structure, with its lower weight toward markets in industrialized countries since 1996, may need revamping in the future.

Figure 2.8
Korea's Share of the Japanese Import Market

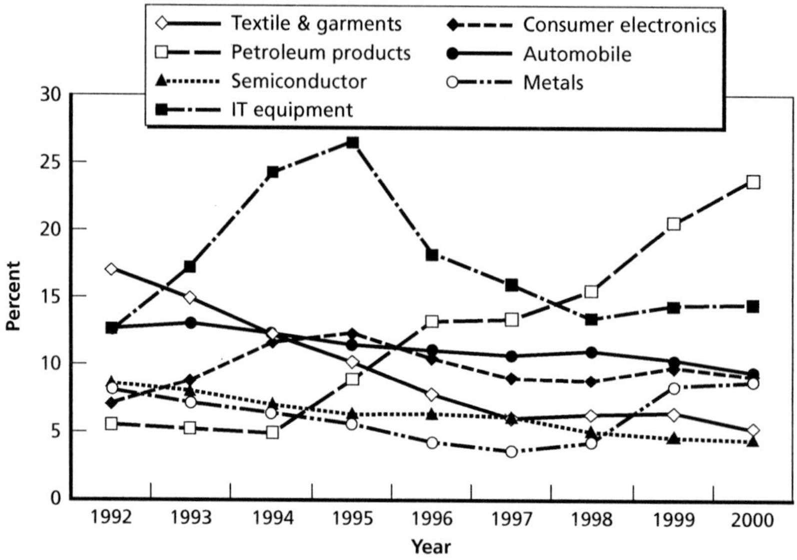

SOURCE: KDI (2003).
RAND *MG320-2.8*

Squeezed Out of the China Market?

In general, Korean companies are under pressure to find their way in the world market in the midst of growing competitiveness from both indigenous Chinese companies and foreign companies in China. Korean companies compete not only with domestic Chinese companies but also with world-class companies operating in China. According to OECD (2002), foreign companies' shares of China's exports and imports were 45.5 percent and 51.8 percent, respectively, in 1999. Korea has a niche in the Chinese market in terms of price competitiveness. However, this niche might be harder to maintain as competition in the Chinese component and equipment market increases. A combination of advanced technologies from the world's leading companies and China's cheap and disciplined labor may create new markets both in China and the world and remove Korea from the market niche it now enjoys.[9] Similar logic can be applied in other products and technologies.

For example, Korea's investment in China contributed to the growth in its exports to China. In 2002, Korean companies in China purchased 38.5 percent of their supplies from Korea whereas their exports to Korea accounted for only 15.8 percent of their sales.[10] As competition in the Chinese component and equipment market increases and as local sourcing of Korean companies in China grows, Korea will probably experience a slowdown in its exports to China.[11]

Is Korea's Manufacturing Sector Being Hollowed Out?

As China becomes a manufacturing powerhouse, the hollowing out of Korea's manufacturing sector is often discussed as one of the threats from China. The story usually goes as follows: China is a "black hole" that absorbs investment and business activities. This might induce a hollowing-out of the manufacturing sector and an exodus of jobs from Korea.[12]

This argument seems plausible to many in Korea's business sector as well as the media. Surveys by business associations usually show that a significant percentage of the respondents believe hollowing-out to be a realistic possibility. Newspapers report the increasing vacancy rate in industrial complexes and the painful lives of people who have lost jobs. According to an article in the *Seoul Economic Daily*, a survey

---

[9] Korean world-class companies, such as Samsung Electronics, LG Electronics, and Hyundai Automobile, are extensively engaged in the Chinese market. However, in our discussions, executives of those leading Korean companies were no exception to the worries over foreign competition in the China market,

[10] KITA (2004).

[11] According to KITA (2004), local sourcing by Korean companies in China averaged 44.3 percent in 2002.

[12] *Hollowing-out* was originally a journalistic term. It usually means that investment, production facilities, and therefore job opportunities in a given sector leave one country and go to others, significantly reducing the first country's economic activities in that sector.

of 1500 Korean companies invested in China, Indonesia, and Vietnam in November 2002 showed that 45 percent of the companies were closing down their factories in Korea, 30 percent had transferred their production facilities overseas, and only 25 percent of them had maintained their domestic factories after their overseas investment.[13] As a consequence, 38.9 percent of the factory sites are now used for other purposes.

However, other studies, including Park and Yang (2004) and Shin et al. (2003), argue that there is not enough evidence to show that the investment rush to China has caused a hollowing out of Korea's manufacturing sector. The decline in domestic production is limited to a few traditional industries, such as textiles and garments, shoes, and consumer electronics. Even though electronics and communication equipment were responsible for more than 30 percent of Korean direct investment outflow in 2003, domestic production in those sectors has been growing fast.

Owing to fast growth in other high-tech manufacturing sectors, the share of manufacturing value-added in nominal GDP has been stable and was still 28 percent as of 2003. When per capita income in the United States and Japan was about $10,000, their shares of manufacturing in GDP were 22.8 percent (1977) and 28.2 percent (1980), respectively. Therefore, Korea's manufacturing sector can hardly be considered weak. Korea's share of manufacturing in total employment has been declining since its peak of 28.8 percent in 1988: Employment in the manufacturing sector is 19.5 percent of total employment as of 2002.[14] Given the stable share in value-added, the declining share of manufacturing in total employment reflects increasing labor productivity.

Hollowing-out might be an exaggeration when applied to Korea's manufacturing sector at present. However, we cannot afford to take the impact of China lightly. Together with Hong Kong and Taiwan, Korea has actively explored new opportunities in China and

---

[13] *Seoul Economic Daily,* 12 January 2004.

[14] Figures are from the databases of the Korea National Statistics Office and Bank of Korea.

enjoyed their benefits. Because of this close economic relationship with China, the effect from possible shocks or slowdowns in China's economy would not be light either.

The Threat May Have Been Covered Up by the Past Decade's World Economic Boom

The competitive pressure from an ascending China may have been relatively weak because the world economy has been booming since the 1990s, with a strong U.S. economy and the explosive growth of China. But in the event of a recession—because of an economic downturn in China, high oil prices, or other reasons—the once-positive relationship between Korea and China could easily turn negative.

In boom times, countries are more cooperative with each other. However, when recession comes, they tend to blame each other for their difficulties. Smaller countries are more vulnerable to the shocks of recession because they get a smaller piece of a smaller pie. Is the pendulum in Korea swinging toward boom or toward bust? Even in the United States in the 1970s and 1980s, the hollowing-out argument was popular as industries moved their assembly processes to countries with cheaper labor, especially in Asia. "Japan bashing" was a term frequently used by journalists in the United States. Of course, in the 1990s, the U.S. economy was booming, with explosive innovations such as the so-called internet revolution—and hollowing-out stories were already forgotten. In 2003, manufacturing made up only 12.7 percent of GDP and 11.3 percent of employment in the United States.[15]

The United States also had to wait for more than ten years to graduate from the fear of being hollowed out. During the 1980s, the

---

[15] The GDP share data are from an article in a monthly journal published by the Bureau of Economic Analysis, Moyer et al. (2004). The employment share is from the Bureau of Labor Statistics Web site, http://data.bls.gov/servlet/SurveyOutputServlet?&series_id=ENUUS00010010&series_id=ENUUS0001051013, accessed 21 November 2004.

United States went through painful layoffs, corporate restructuring, and organizational innovations before it bloomed again in the 1990s with IT innovations and a booming economy that produced high growth and low inflation. It is important to understand that the backbone of this successful yet painful restructuring was a highly developed market system and an absolute advantage in science, technology, and knowledge.

Taiwan is a more recent example. Taiwan started investing aggressively in China earlier than Korea. The hollowing-out stories sounded persuasive in Taiwan because the Taiwanese economy has lost a significant number of manufacturing jobs in the last decade and its economy was slow until 2003—ever since the Asian economic crisis. The impact of Taiwan's second surge of investment in China between 2000 and 2003 was especially significant. Anticipating China's membership in the World Trade Organization (WTO), Taiwan increased its investment in China after 2000. Taiwan's unemployment rate surged from less than 3 percent in 2000 to almost 5 percent in 2003. Of course, this increase may not be totally due to investment in China, but it is known that more than 50 percent of Taiwan's IT products are assembled in offshore production facilities.[16]

As with Korea, a significant part of Taiwanese exports to China go to Taiwanese factories in China for final assembly and reexport to the United States and other countries. When Taiwan started to record higher export and economic growth rates, talk about the negative side of a rising China became subdued both there and in other countries. But, regardless of its truthfulness, worry about hollowing out may come up again if recession hits—whether it starts in China, the United States, or elsewhere.

---

[16] See Chase, Pollpeter, and Mulvenon (2004) for further discussion on the hollowing-out controversies in Taiwan.

External Risk Factors: China's Overheated Economy

Given the structural weaknesses remaining in Korea after the 1997 crisis, Korea is also watching out for external and internal shocks caused by China's record-breaking growth and expansion in the world economy. The Chinese government seems to be taking note of the alarming signs of overheating in the Chinese economy.[17] Many experts believe the possibility of an abrupt collapse of the Chinese economy is small. China is aiming to decrease its GDP growth rate from 9.1 percent in 2003 to 7 percent in 2004. However, it is too early to tell whether the measures taken by the Chinese government will be sufficient to cool down the overheated economy and let China enter into a slow, mild recession—a so-called soft landing.

As China's economic weight has increased, its economic performance and stability have become important for other countries, especially for Asian countries, including Korea, that have a close economic relationship with China. For example, in 2003 Korean companies had to compete with Chinese companies to get enough raw materials, such as iron and steel and even container ships, needed for production and export.[18] Shortages of raw materials used to exist only within China, but now they are a problem for other countries as well, including Korea. It goes without saying that China's economic performance would have a much greater influence in times of recession, considering Korea's heavy engagement in the China market. How resources are deployed in China will have a great effect on the Korean economy.

---

[17] The People's Bank of China increased its reserve requirement between September 2003 and April 2004. On April 25, 2004, the central bank increased the reserve requirement from 7 percent to 7.5 percent and announced a target of decreasing the new loans by 13 percent to $314 billion in 2004. In March 2004, Premier Wen Jiabao also said that government bonds for infrastructure construction would be decreased by 25 percent in 2004.

[18] For example, metal prices were soaring in 2003 partly due to China's construction boom in buildings, factories, and telecommunication systems and other infrastructure. China became the first country ever to import more than $1 billion of American scrap metal in 2003. See Andrew Pollack and Keith Bradsher, "China's Need for Metal Keeps U.S. Scrap Dealers Scrounging," *New York Times,* 13 March 2004.

As with other rapidly growing developing nations, China is not free from structural vulnerabilities that are easily covered up by fast growth. Korea and other Asian countries have already seen that their structural weaknesses can be exposed by external shocks, bringing a surprisingly quick economic crisis.

Narrowing Technological Gap Between Korea and China

Much of the Korean unease about China stems from the relative progress in technological capability of the two countries. Science and technological capability is a major determinant of current and future competitiveness in world markets. China is catching up with Korea in areas of Korea's technological strength, just as Korea is catching up with Japan. Many studies predict that the technological gap between Japan, Korea, and China will narrow considerably in the near future. One of Korea's main concerns is narrowing the technological gap between Korea and China. Thus, in the next chapter we examine Korea's S&T capability relative to that of China.

CHAPTER THREE

Current Technological Capability: S&T Indicators and Trends

In this chapter, we evaluate the present S&T capability of China and Korea and examine major trends of science and technology progress in the two countries. We first analyze existing aggregate S&T capacity indices for Korea and China compared with the rest of the world. Then we compare Korea and China in terms of R&D input and output indicators, such as R&D investment, human resources, patents, copyrights, and publication of science and engineering papers.

We address the following topics: How do the aggregate S&T capability measures evaluate the S&T potential of Korea and China in comparison with other countries? What are the relative weaknesses and strengths of each country as reflected in major S&T indicators? What would be the impacts of the major trends on the future of S&T progress in China?

International Comparison of Technological Capabilities

How are the current S&T capabilities of Korea and China evaluated in comparison with those of other countries? Is there any quantified aggregate measure to show how capable each country is in S&T compared with the rest of the world?

Country-Level Aggregate Indices of S&T Capabilities

A number of studies have attempted to measure country-level aggregate S&T capabilities. The UNDP's Technological Achievement Index (TAI), the ArCo index of SPRU, RAND's Science and Technological Capacity Index (STCI), OECD's Science, Technology and Industry (STI) Scoreboard, and the competitiveness indices of IMD and the World Economic Forum (WEF) are among them.

The STI Scoreboard analyzes a wide range of indicators across four dimensions: creation and diffusion of knowledge, information economy, global integration, and economic structure and productivity. But it does not provide one aggregated S&T capability for each country. The IMD's *World Competitiveness Yearbook* produces aggregate capability indices such as science competitiveness indices and rankings among difference countries. The IMD competitiveness index depends on survey methods together with objective data.

TAI, the ArCo Index, and STCI focus more on knowledge creation, diffusion, and usage, and they are constructed using objective statistics without depending on surveys.[1] These three indices vary in details but are similar in the scope of their analysis and their analytical method.

TAI, the ArCo Index, and STCI often use indicators of R&D resources, outcomes, and infrastructure as proxy variables to represent knowledge creation, diffusion, and usage.[2] The indicators that are aggregated into the weighting scheme of each capability index are shown in Table 3.1. Depending on what individual indicators were included and how they were weighted in the aggregate index, the country rankings of the countries vary a little.

---

[1] Existing literature on technology-level comparison based on survey method will be introduced later in Chapter Five. As an objective assessment of technological capability, the surveys were subject to substantial limitations We discuss this issue more in detail later.

[2] For the details of the studies, refer to Archibugi and Coco (2004), UNDP (2001), Wagner et al. (2000), and Wagner, Horlings, and Dutta (2003).

Table 3.1
Comparison of TAI, ArCo Index, and STCI

	TAI	ArCo Index	STCI
Objective	To capture how well a country as a whole is participating in creating and diffusing technology and building human skill base	To measure country-level technological capabilities by building upon TAI and other existing literature	To compare inputs and capacities of countries to conduct scientific and technical research
Main components	Creation of technology Diffusion of new technology Diffusion of old technology Human skills	Creation of technology Technological infrastructure Development of human skills	**Enabling factors** that help create environment conducive to the absorption, retention, production and diffusion of knowledge **Resources** that can be devoted to S&T activities that concern indicators relating most directly to S&T capacity **Embedded knowledge** of science and technology, and the extent to which researchers are connected to the global scientific community
Data and proxy variables	Patents granted per capita Receipts of royalty and license fees from abroad per capita Internet hosts per capita	Patents Scientific articles, Internet penetration	R&D as percentage of GDP Tertiary science enrollment Number of scientists and engineers

Table 3. 1—continued

	TAI	ArCo Index	STCI
Data and proxy variables	High- and medium-technology exports as a share of all exports Logarithm of electricity consumption per capita Mean years of schooling Gross enrollment ratio of tertiary level in science, mathematics, and engineering	Electricity consumption Tertiary science and engineering enrollment Mean years of schooling Literacy rate	Number of institutions R&D expenditure Coauthorship index external patenting activity S&T journal articles
Number of countries analyzed	72	162	76
Results (country groups and member countries)	Leaders: 18 Potential leaders: 19 Dynamic adopters: 26 Marginalized: 9	Leaders: 25 Potential leaders: 25 Latecomers: 61 Marginalized: 51	Scientifically advanced countries: 16 Scientifically proficient countries: 11 Scientifically developing countries: 40 Lagging countries: 9
Korea's position	In 1st group, "leaders"; ranks 5th	In 1st group, "leaders"; ranks 19th	In 2nd group, "scientifically proficient countries"; ranks 18th
China's position	In 3rd group, "dynamic adopters"; ranks 45th	In 3rd group, "latecomers"; ranks 85th	In 3rd group, "scientifically developing countries"; ranks 47th
Rankings of other countries	Finland, 1st United States, 2nd Japan, 4th UK, 7th Germany, 11th	Sweden, 1st Finland, 2nd United States, 5th Japan, 8th Germany, 12th UK, 13th	United States, 1st Japan, 6th Germany, 7th UK, 11th

Korea Is Currently Ahead of China in Aggregate S&T Capability

The aggregate indices of TAI, ArCo Index, and STCI all show that Korea's aggregate score of S&T capacity is higher than that of China.[3] The STCI shows that Korea belongs in the second-tier group and ranks 18th out of 76 countries, as shown in Table 3.1. According to the TAI and ArCo index, Korea belongs to the top group in S&T and ranks 5th and 19th out of 72 countries and 172 countries respectively, whereas China belongs to the third group and ranks 45th and 85th, respectively.

Interestingly, Korea is ahead of the United Kingdom, Germany, and France on the TAI. This may be because TAI was built on proxies that include Internet hosts per capita and the ratio of high- and medium-technology exports to all exports— areas where Korea would earn high scores.

High R&D-to-GDP Ratio and High Gross Tertiary Science Enrollment Are the Major Contributors to Korea's High STCI Score

The STCI shows the contribution of individual indicators. For Korea, as we see in Figure 3.1, gross tertiary science enrollment and R&D as a percentage of GDP contributed greatly to Korea's score while number of research institutes, number of S&T journal articles, and coauthorship indicators contributed negatively to Korea's rank.

Korea's R&D-to-GDP ratio was 2.91 percent in 2002, which is close to those of Japan (3.09 percent in 2001) and the United States (2.82 percent in 2002) but far below those of Sweden (4.27 percent in 2001) and Finland (3.40 percent in 2001). China's R&D as a percentage of GDP was 1.23 percent in 2002 (Table 3.2).

Gross tertiary science enrollment ratio data are from UNDP (2001). This ratio is defined as the number of students enrolled in tertiary education in science, regardless of age, as a percentage of the population of the relevant age range. Korea's gross tertiary science enrollment ratio between 1995 and 1997 was 23.2 percent. Accord-

---

[3] IMD's SCI Science Competitiveness Index also shows that Korea is more capable than China.

Figure 3.1
Contribution of Individual Indicators to the STCI Score: Scientifically Proficient Countries

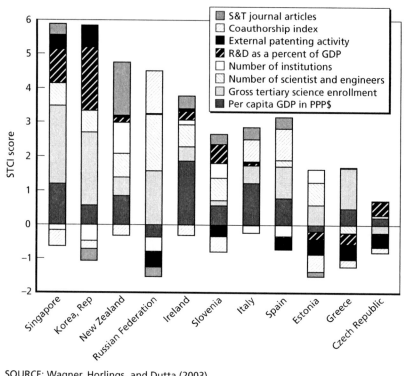

SOURCE: Wagner, Horlings, and Dutta (2003).
RAND *MG320-3.1*

ing to UNDP (2001), only Finland (27.4) and Singapore (24.2) had higher ratios than Korea.

More-current statistics from OECD show that Korea's ratio of scientists and engineers to total higher education degree holders was 41 percent in 2003, higher than Japan's 29.2 percent and the United States' 18.0 percent.[4] This statistic looks paradoxical because "avoid-

---

[4] KITA (2004). The original source is OECD's Education Online Database.

ance of science and technology majors" has been often highlighted as a critical economic and social problems in Korea.

However, the density of scientist and engineers in the total population is much lower in Korea than in the United States or Japan, reflecting a lower ratio of highly educated people to the total population in Korea. The number of researchers per 10,000 population in Korea, Japan, and the United States is 39.9 (2002), 53.1 (2001), and 45.2 (1999) respectively. If people's preferences are rational, promoting higher education itself might be a solution for Korea's lack of high-quality scientists and engineers, if any.[5]

Limitations of Aggregate Indices

The rankings in the aggregate S&T capacity indices must be interpreted carefully. China's lower ranking on the TAI, ArCo index, and STCI in comparison with Korea does not necessarily mean that China's absolute S&T capability or potential is inferior to Korea's. Many individual indicators used in constructing the aggregate capacity indices were standardized by population size or GDP. Therefore, intensity rather than absolute size matters in the measures of technological capability shown above.

In a stylized analysis of international comparison of S&T indicators, it is often necessary and useful to control for difference in the size of the economy and the population. However, if the analysis focuses on each country's technological capability or on comparing the technological strengths of two countries, as our analysis does, the size of R&D expenditure and the absolute number of scientists and engineers are more relevant indicators. We keep this aspect in mind in the following analysis.

The three technological capability measures discussed above do not take into consideration the knowledge stock that each country

---

[5] The authors suspect that the mismatch of supply and demand in terms of qualifications and technology fields might often be expressed as a shortage of scientists and engineers in general. If there were a real shortage in general, relative compensation for scientists and engineers should have improved. Ironically, the issue of "avoidance of scientist and engineers" in Korea is usually discussed in parallel with relatively low compensation for scientists and engineers.

already has. For example, although Korea is relatively strong in commercialization technology, China may have inherited accumulated
knowledge in basic science and defense-related technology, such as
nuclear physics, material science, remote sensing, aerospace and satellite technology, from its Communist era. But this accumulated
knowledge stock was not counted in the existing technological capability indices since those indices are mainly based on flow indicators—for example, R&D expenditure and GDP.

On an Absolute Scale, China Is Ahead in R&D Investment and Human Resources[6]

Because of its vast population, China is often put in the less capable
group in terms of per capita S&T indicators. However, in terms of its
collective power and its reach as a nation, it is often among the
world's leading nations. This is also true in a comparison of S&T capabilities.

As we see from Table 3.2, while the R&D intensity of Korea is
more than twice as high as that of China, China's absolute level of
R&D expenditure is 10 percent higher than Korea's. If we consider
purchasing power parity (PPP), China's R&D expenditures are three
times those of Korea.[7] Also, the number of scientists and engineers

---

[6] R&D expenditure data in this report include both civil R&D and defense R&D, unless
otherwise specified. However, data to break R&D down into defense and nondefense components were not available. For Korea, we can infer indirectly the share of defense R&D.
The Korea Ministry of Defense accounts for 13.2 percent (about $720 million) of the total
government R&D budget in 2004. Assuming the ratio of government-funded R&D to total
R&D in 2004 is the same as it was in 2003 and that other ministries and the nongovernment sector are not involved in defense R&D, we can infer that the share of defense R&D in
total R&D in Korea is about 2.9 percent. This contrasts sharply with the United States,
where the R&D budget of the Department of Defense is $48.5 billion, accounting for 16.6
percent of total R&D in 2002.

[7] Purchasing power parity (PPP) is a currency conversion rate that both convert to a common currency and equalizes the purchasing power of different currencies. In other words,
PPP conversion eliminates the differences in price levels between countries. Comparative
price levels are often defined as the ratio of PPP to exchange rate. For our analysis of R&D,
it would be ideal if we could apply PPP for R&D goods only instead of PPP for total private
final consumption expenditure. Since PPP data are not available for R&D goods, we are
assuming the two PPPs are the same. The two PPPs might actually be quite different from
each other in a country like China, where partitions exist between sectors—for example, the

Table 3.2
Major Indicators, Korea and China, 2002

	China (A)	Korea (B)	A/B
Land	9,596,900 km^2	99,585 km^2	96.7
Population	1,284.5 million	47.6 million	27.0
GDP	$1,237,100 million	$546,886 million	2.3
Exchange rate / PPP	4.7	1.7	2.7
Total R&D expenditure	$15,600 million (100.0%)	$13,847 million (100.0%)	1.1
Basic research	$891 million (5.7%)	$1,897 million (13.7%)	0.5
Applied research	$2,980 million (19.2%)	$3,008 million (21.7%)	1.0
Development	$11,685 million (75.1%)	$8,942 million (64.6%)	1.3
Government-funded R&D	$3,612 million[a] (33.4%)	$3,074 million (22.2%)	NA
Non-government and non–foreign-funded R&D	$ 6,923 million[a] (64.0%)	$10,712 million (77.4%)	NA
Foreign-funded R&D	$290 million[a] (2.3%)	$61.0 million (0.4%)	NA
Scientists and engineers (full-time equivalents)	742,001	141,001	5.2
SCI[b] papers	40,785	17,785	2.0
R&D/GDP	1.23	2.91	0.4
Scientists and engineers per 10,000 population	16 (2001)	39.9	0.4

SOURCE: OECD (2004), KMOST (2003 and 2004), Korea National Bureau of Statistics, World Bank Web site, CMOST (2003c), Korea Trade Association Web site.

NOTE: Exchange rates of 8.2773 RMB/dollar and 1251.2 won/dollar were applied to change amounts in Chinese and Korean currency into dollars. Hong Kong and Macao are included in SCI's count of China's papers (CMOST, 2003b). Defense R&D is included in the R&D expenditure. Data for the breakdown between nondefense and defense R&D are not available.

[a] Data for China's R&D by funding source (government, nongovernment, and foreign) are from CMOST (2003b) for 2000.

[b] SCI = Science Citation Index.

---

market economy and the centrally planned economy, the rural sector and the urban sector. As we discuss later, China has a large cadre of graduate students who act as low-cost, high-quality research workers, for example. This factor would increase China's PPP for R&D. Therefore, we use the PPP-based comparison as a reference point only and discuss it together with absolute expenditure.

per 10,000 population in Korea is 2.5 times that of China, while the absolute number of scientist and engineers of China is seven times that of Korea. Foreign R&D investment in China (2000) is almost five times that in Korea (2002). China's vast human resources, fast growth in R&D expenditure, and excellence in some areas of basic science, mean that it may well have greater S&T potential than Korea. Since China is so large in terms of population and geographic area compared with Korea (Korea has less than 4 percent of China's population and 1 percent of its geographical area), a one-to-one comparison of China and Korea at the aggregated country level must be complemented with a more micro-level comparison and analysis.

The comparison would be quite different if we compared Korea to the east coast provinces of China where most of China's technological development has taken place. The R&D intensity of east coast China is much higher than that of the country as a whole. However, given that China's R&D expenditures are presently only 10 percent more than Korea's, it still makes sense to compare the two at the country level. In terms of R&D and economy size, Korea and China are comparable at present. Of course, this may change in the long-term future if China's economy continues to grow as rapidly as before.

Major S&T Indicators for China

In recent years, China has shown impressive progress in various S&T input and output indicators.

Rapid Growth in R&D Investment

China's gross expenditure on R&D (GERD) had been growing rapidly, which is not surprising for China, where almost all indicators are changing rapidly. As shown in Table 3.3, China's GERD more than doubled between 1997 and 2002. The compounded annual growth rate (CAGR) of GERD reached 20 percent per annum. In 2002,

Table 3.3
Selected S&T Indicators, China, 1997–2002

	1997	1998	1999	2000	2001	2002	CAGR[c] (1997–2002)
National S&T Financing Indicators[a]							
GERD (US $million)	6,152	6,659	8,203	10,822	12,596	15,557	20%
GERD/GDP (%)	0.64	0.69	0.83	1.01	1.09	1.23	14%
Government S&T appropriation (US $million)	4,940	5,299	6,572	6,955	8,497	9,862	15%
Government S&T appropriation/total government expenditure (%)	4.4	4.1	4.1	3.6	3.7	3.7	N/A
R&D Personnel Indicators							
R&D personnel (1000 FTEs)	831.2	755.2	821.7	925.4	956.5	1035.1	4%
Scientists and engineers (1000 FTEs)	588.7	485.5	531.1	698	742.7	810.5	7%
S&T Output Indicators							
Number of patent applications (cases in China)	114,208	121,989	134,239	170,682	203,573	252,631	17%
S&T papers catalogued by SCI, ISTP and EI[b]	35,311	35,003	46,188	49,678	64,526	77,395	17%
Exports of high-tech products (US $billion)	16.3	20.3	24.7	37.0	46.5	67.9	33%
Percentage of high-tech products in total exports	8.9	11	12.7	14.9	17.5	20.8	19%

SOURCE: CMOST (2003b)
[a] Exchange rate of 8.276 RMB/dollar applied.
[b] SCI = Science Citation Index, IS&TP = Index to Scientific and Technical Proceedings, EI = Engineering Index.
[c] CAGR calculated by the authors.

China spent $15.6 billion on R&D, which is comparable to Korea's GERD of US $13.8 billion.[8] In terms of PPP, China's R&D expenditure could be worth $73.2 billion, 3.1 times that of Korea's $23.5 billion.[9]

Relatively Little Funding for Basic Research

Investment in basic research is often used as a proxy for future oriented research activities and long-term innovation capabilities. Industrial countries usually spend between 14 and 22 percent of R&D funding on basic research.

In 2002, China's R&D expenditures were allocated largely to development activities (75 percent). Only 5.7 percent of China's R&D expenditures went to basic research, compared with Korea's 13.7 percent and the United States' 18.1 percent.

Scientific Paper Publication Outperforms Basic Research Investment

Basic science capacity is often measured by number of scientific papers published. According to SCI data, China published twice as many science papers as Korea in 2002 and ranked sixth in the world in terms of number of publications.

On the input side however, China's investment in basic science is only half of Korea's, as Table 3.2 shows. With half the investment, China publishes twice as many science papers as Korea does. Even if we consider the fact that China's purchasing power was 2.7 times that of Korea's in 2002, China is investing only 1.35 times as much as Korea but publishing twice as many papers.

Why does China's scientific paper publication outperform its investment for basic research? One of the reasons is that China has abundant human resources for R&D in universities and research institutes—resources that can be tapped at marginal or sometimes no extra cost. Graduate students often serve as low-cost researchers, and

---

[8] The United States spent $292.2 billion on R&D in 2002, which is almost 20 times as much as China.

[9] Here again, we assume that the PPP for R&D goods is the same as PPP for private final private consumption for both Korea and China.

there were more than 500,000 graduate students enrolled in China in 2002—nearly twice as many as in Korea, which has 262,867.[10]

Another reason may lie in the difference in accumulated knowledge stock in basic science. R&D investment is a flow variable, so the number of science papers per unit of investment does not capture this difference in knowledge stock. In addition, like other socialist countries, China has emphasized the importance of so-called big sciences, such as aerospace, nuclear science, oceanography, and other basic sciences; even now, this tradition continues to some extent in the context of national security.

In our analysis of S&T indicators, we examined flow data as other experts in this field do, because comparable data for stock variables such as knowledge stock are not available. However, the performance of basic research will depend not only on R&D investment but also on the existing stock of knowledge as well as other factors.

Korean and Chinese papers are cited less than papers by American authors, averaging four and three citations, respectively (Table 3.4). According to ISI Essential Science Indicators,[11] which covers the ten-year period from January 1993 to August 31, 2003, China ranked 9th and Korean ranked 16th, based on the number of papers catalogued by SCI in all fields. In terms of the total number of citations, China ranked 19th while Korea dropped out of the top 20 during the period.

China's publication growth rate is also much higher than Korea's. Although there are concerns that a majority of China's researchers are not yet world-leading thinkers and that the Chinese R&D results are not as influential as those of the world's leading researchers,[12]

---

[10] Data were obtained from KMEHRD (2004) and CMOE (2002).

[11] "The Year 2003: Top 20 Country Rankings in All Fields," Thompson InCites, ISI Essential Science Indicators, covering a period of ten years plus eight months, January 1993–August 31, 2003, online at http://in-cites.com/countries/2003allfields.html, accessed 20 October 2004.

[12] Ray Wu (2000), "China Faces Challenges in Improving Its Output Efficiency in Scientific Research," *China Voices* (Supplement to *Nature*) 426 (6968), 18/25 December 2003 (in Chinese), online at www.natureasia.com/ch/webfocus/chinavoices/RayWu.php, accessed 20 September 2004.

Table 3.4
**World Rankings of Selected Countries for Papers
Catalogued by SCI, January 1993–August 2003**

Rank	Country	Papers	Citations	Citations per Paper
1	United States	2,705,352	33,089,756	12
2	Japan	713,542	5,098,499	7
3	Germany	655,586	5,857,244	9
4	England	598,470	6,212,840	10
5	France	484,291	4,213,581	9
6	Canada	358,007	3,549,116	10
7	Italy	310,557	2,569,970	8
8	Russia	285,856	848,345	3
9	China	236,996	658,355	3
10	Australia	211,549	1,736,998	8
16	South Korea	111,406	420,349	4

SOURCE: "The Year 2003: Top 20 Country Rankings in All Fields," Thompson InCites, ISI Essential Science Indicators covering a ten-year-plus-eight-month period, January 1993–August 31, 2003, available from http://in-cites.com/countries/2003allfields.html, accessed 20 October 2004.

NOTE: Rankings are based on number of papers, not citation frequency.

China has made consistent and rapid progress in recent years not just in the quantity but also in the quality of papers published.

Some Studies Assert That China Is Already a "Research Powerhouse"
Chinese S&T output indicators, such as scientific and technical papers catalogued by SCI, ISTP, and EI, have been increasing at a CAGR of 17 percent per annum (see Table 3.3). China ranked sixth in papers catalogued by SCI, and fifth in papers catalogued by SCI, EI, and ISTP, suggesting that China is one of the front-runners in research. As long as rankings are based on number of papers, these studies will reach similar conclusions. All in all, China has more than one million R&D personnel and more than five times as many scientists and engineers as Korea has (refer to Table 3.1).

For example, Porter et al. (2002) calculated the "national emerging technology ranks" based on national R&D publications in selected fields in 1999. Referring to Popper et al. (1998), the study selected the following fields as representatives for emerging technologies: software, optical communications, computer hardware, advanced materials for computing/communication technologies, and biotechnology.

According to the index of Porter et al. (2002), China ranked 5th, 4th, 6th, 4th, and 7th respectively, in these fields with an overall ranking of 5th. The study put China in the same category as Germany, the United Kingdom, and France as "research powerhouses," behind the "superpowers" of the United States and Japan. In the same study, Korea ranked 18th, 7th, 11th, 7th and 8th respectively with an overall ranking of 8th. The result put Korea in the group of "strong players":

- Superpowers: United States and Japan
- Research powerhouses: Germany, United Kingdom, China, and France
- Strong players: Italy, Korea, Canada, Russia, and Taiwan.

Of course, a country's high-tech capabilities cannot be reduced to a few indicators. However, performance indicators such as SCI, EI and ISTP and their level and growth all point to the fact that China has a significant research capability at present and it could become a major research power in the near future. This is not surprising if we again recognize the abundance of its human resources both for manufacturing and research.

At present, China's research potential seems to be better utilized by foreign companies than by indigenous Chinese companies. We discuss this phenomenon later in our analysis of patent activities and the increasing number of foreign research laboratories in China.

Figure 3.2
Number of Papers Published on Six Emerging Technologies, Selected Countries, 1999

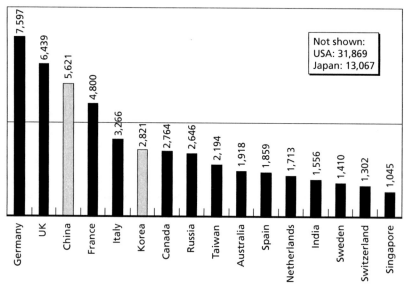

Not shown:
USA: 31,869
Japan: 13,067

Germany 7,597
UK 6,439
China 5,621
France 4,800
Italy 3,266
Korea 2,821
Canada 2,764
Russia 2,646
Taiwan 2,194
Australia 1,918
Spain 1,859
Netherlands 1,713
India 1,556
Sweden 1,410
Switzerland 1,302
Singapore 1,045

SOURCE: Porter et al. (2002).
RAND *MG320-3.2*

China Has an Absolute Advantage in Scientists and Engineers, and the Supply Is Abundant and Increasing

China currently ranks second in the world in number of R&D personnel. It has more doctoral degree holders than Japan, and its number of persons who have completed higher education in the S&T field is close to that of the United States.[13]

China's full-time-equivalent R&D personnel was over one million as of 2002, second only to that of the United States and roughly

---

[13] "World Manufacturing–China Is a Workshop, Not a Factory Yet," *Xinhua News*, 25 April 2004, online at http://news.xinhuanet.com/fortune/2004-04/25/content_ 1439250.htm, accessed 12 September 2004.

six times that of Korea.[14] However, China's ratio of R&D personnel to per 10,000 workers is only one-fifth of Korea's. Given the vast population base of China and low R&D intensity of the industrial sector, this figure is not surprising.

Between 1997 and 2002, the number of R&D personnel in China grew at a CAGR of 4 percent per annum, significantly higher than its population growth rate of 0.77 percent during the same period.[15] The number of scientists and engineers engaging in R&D has also been increasing at a CAGR of 7 percent per annum (see Table 3.3).

Success in Educational Reform Further Strengthens China's Human Resource Advantage

The Chinese government has introduced major educational reforms since it has declared "rejuvenating the nation through science and education" to be its fundamental national development strategy in 1995.[16] The government education budget almost doubled between 1997 and 2002 to US $40.7 billion. The education budget increased from 2.5 percent of GDP to 3.3 percent in the same period.

The investment and reforms in the education system have helped China to make impressive progress.[17] The improvement in education is especially notable in higher education—the main source of S&T personnel.

The number of registered students in higher education increased by 250 percent between 1990 and 2002 (Table 3.5). Similar, albeit less dramatic, increases occurred for students registered in senior and junior high schools during the same period.

---

[14] Data from CMOE (2002) and KITA (2004).

[15] Calculated by the authors from *China Statistical Year Book* 2003.

[16] Reform programs in higher education will be discussed in the next chapter.

[17] See Zhu (2003) and Cohen and Soto (2001).

Table 3.5
Number of Enrolled Students per 10,000 Population in China, 1990–2002

Year	Higher Education	Senior High School	Junior High School	Primary School	Kindergarten
1990	326	1,337	3,426	10,707	1,725
1995	457	1,610	3,945	11,010	2,262
2000	723	2,018	4,969	10,335	1,782
2001	931	2,021	5,161	9,937	1,602
2002	1,146	2,283	5,240	9,525	1,595

SOURCE: CMOE (2003).

Another salient feature of the Chinese education system is that it has a high percentage of science and engineering (including medicine and agriculture) students, although the percentage seemed to be decreasing during the period. As of 2001, the share of science and engineering major in total enrollment in higher education was 55 percent (Table 3.6), higher than most developed and newly industrializing countries.[18] The ratio was 45 percent in Korea as of 2003.[19]

Table 3.6
Number of Registered (Enrolled) Students in China's Universities and Junior Colleges

Subject	1995	2000	2001
Science and engineering	1,842,628	3,289,802	3,922,901
Social sciences and others	1,063,801	2,271,098	3,267,757
Total students in higher education	2,906,429	5,560,900	7,190,658
Percentage of science and engineering students in total	63%	59%	55%

SOURCE: China National Bureau of Statistics (NBS), *China Statistical Year Book,* 1996, 2001, and 2002 editions.

---

[18] OECD (2002a).

[19] KMEHRD (2004).

The Chinese education system is expected to provide China with an increasing number of well-trained scientists and engineers for many years to come. In 2002, the total number of students enrolled in China's higher education institutions reached 9.5 million, approximately 3.2 times that of Korea's.

According to China's tenth five-year education plan, under-graduate enrollment in China will overtake that in the United States by 2010.[20] In 2000, the United States had 15.3 million students enrolled in higher education, and its average annual growth rate in enrollment between 1990 and 2000 was 1 percent per year.[21]

The U.S. National Center for Education Statistics projects that total undergraduate enrollment will increase by 23 percent between 2000 and 2013, from 15.3 million to 18.8 million.[22] China's tenth five-year education plan projects 23 million undergraduates and one million postgraduates enrolled in universities by 2010.[23] Therefore, China may overtake the United States in undergraduate enrollment by 2010.

Patent Data Show China Has Limited Invention Capabilities

Patent application in China and U.S. patent awards to Chinese nationals suggest that China is still a country with relatively low capabilities in invention and innovation.

In terms of growth rate, China has been highly active in patenting. Between 1998 and 2002, the number of all patents filed at the China State Intellectual Property Office (CSIPO) grew at CAGR

---

[20] "China's University Students to Exceed 16 Million by 2005," *China Daily*, 29 March 2001, http://english.people.com.cn/english/200103/29/eng20010329_66329.html, accessed 19 August 2004.

[21] Calculated by the author from "Digest of Education Statistics, 2002," National Center for Education Statistics, online at http://nces.ed.gov/programs/digest/d02/index.asp, accessed 20 September 2004.

[22] "Projections of Education Statistics to 2013," U.S. National Center for Education Statistics, online at http://nces.ed.gov//programs/projections/ch_2.asp#2, accessed 20 September 2004.

[23] "The 10th Five Year Plan for Education," Ministry of Education, (in Chinese), online at www.moe.edu.cn/news/2002_06/3.htm, accessed 10 August 2004.

of 20 percent per annum (Table 3.7). Chinese citizens account for 85 percent of the total patents filed; the remaining 15 percent come from foreigners. However, foreign applicants disproportionately file for patent applications in the category of inventions (85 percent), while Chinese citizens mostly file in the categories of utility design and appearance design (Table 3.7). In 2002, only 19.4 percent of total Chinese applications for patents were in the invention category.[24]

Of course, patent statistics are only one of several indicators of innovation capability. Although patents are one of the most frequently used indicators of innovation and technological progress, patent data have limitations as a S&T indicator because not all inventions are patented. Inventors often make a strategic decision to patent rather than to rely on secrecy, lead-time advantages, and the use of complementary marketing and manufacturing capabilities. Because intellectual property rights (IPR) are not well protected in China, Chinese patent counts may undervalue invention in China more than in countries with better IPR protection.

To complement the serious limitations of Chinese domestic patent data, we will examine international patenting activities and analyze technology absorption, which is a crucial part of technological capability in developing countries like China.

Table 3.7
Patents Filed in CSIPO, 2002

Type of Patent	Chinese Citizens (%)	Foreigners (%)	Total
Invention	39,806 (19.4)	40,426 (85.9)	80,232
Utility design	92,166 (44.8)	973 (2.0)	93,139
Appearance design	73,572 (35.8)	5,688 (12.1)	79,260
Total	205,544 (100.0)	47,087 (100.0)	252,631

SOURCE: CSIPO Annual Report, 2002, www.sipo.gov.cn/sipo_English/ndbg/nb/ndbg2002/t20030425_34034.htm, accessed 14 December 2004.

---

[24] See www.sts.org.cn/sjkl/kjtjdt/data2003/2003-4.htm, accessed 30 August 2004.

The Chinese Industrial Sector Is Not the Major Player in Invention-Type Patents

As Table 3.8 shows, universities and research institutes together possess many more valid invention patents than industry does.[25] Chinese universities, research institutes, and government together possessed twice as many valid invention patents as industry as of 2001. Out of valid invention-type patents owned by Chinese institutes (except those possessed by individuals), enterprises had only 24.4 percent, while universities, research institutes, and governments accounted for 75.6 percent. This contrasts sharply with the foreign patenting activities in China, where the lion's share of valid invention patents is owned by enterprises.

China Is Behind in Overseas Patent Activity

U.S. patent statistics show that China is far behind developed countries and other newly industrializing countries including Korea. In 2003, of the total foreign utility patent (i.e., "patents for invention") applications in the United States, Japan had the biggest share with 43.8 percent, followed by Germany with 14.1 percent. Taiwan ranked third with 6.5 percent, followed by Korea with 4.9 percent. China ranked 29th, with only 0.1 percent of the total.

It should be noted that although China's patent applications in the United States had been below 100 per year before 1999, they have increased to over 100 since 2000. In terms of cumulative number of U.S. patents of foreign origin between 1963 and 2003, Japan and Germany are the top two performers, with 38.3 percent and 18.3 percent share of the total, respectively (Table 3.9).

The Technology Review's (TR's) Annual Patent Scorecard ranks the U.S. patent portfolios of 150 top technology companies in eight industries: aerospace; computers; electronics; semiconductors; telecommunications; biotechnology; and pharmaceuticals, chemicals, and

---

[25] A *valid patent* is a patent that has not been terminated or abandoned.

Table 3.8
Valid Invention-Type Patents by Sector, 2001

		Valid Invention-Type Patents (A)					Total Patents (All Types) (B)	A/B (%)
		Institutions				Individuals		
		Universities	R&D Institutes	Firms	Government			
Chinese	Number	1,885	2,879	2,946	1,049	8,552	31,147	55.6
	Percent	10.9	16.6	17.0	6.1	49.4		
Foreign	Number	113	219	26,958	3,567	1,403	46,209	69.8
	Percent	0.4	0.7	83.6	11.1	4.3		

SOURCE: CMOST (2003c), p.129.
NOTE: Patents were counted at the end of year 2001.

Table 3.9
U.S. Utility Patents Granted to Selected Countries, 1998–2003

	1998	1999	2000	2001	2002	2003	% of Total, 2003	Rank in 2003
Total foreign-origin patents	67,229	69,580	72,426	78,432	80,361	81,127		
Japan	30,840	31,104	31,295	33,224	34,859	35,517	43.8%	1
Germany	9,095	9,337	10,235	11,259	11,280	11,444	14.1%	2
Taiwan	3,100	3,693	4,667	5,371	5,431	5,298	6.5%	3
Korea	3,259	3,562	3,314	3,538	3,786	3,944	4.9%	4
France	3,674	3,820	3,819	4,041	4,035	3,869	4.8%	5
UK	3,464	3,572	3,667	3,965	3,837	3,627	4.5%	6
Canada	2,974	3,226	3,419	3,606	3,431	3,426	4.2%	7
China	72	90	119	195	289	297	0.4%	29

SOURCE: U.S. Patent and Trademark Office.
NOTE: The U.S. definition of utility patents is "patents for invention."

automotive.[26] These data provide not only the patent counts for each company but also other indices constructed from the frequency of citation of the patents and links to scientific research. No Chinese company ranked on the TR Patent Scorecard as of 2003.

Of course, patent statistics are only one of several indicators of innovation capability. Technology assimilation and linkage to the global R&D network may be as important as invention capability in China since its economy is still in the development stage.

Korea Is Relatively Strong in International Patent Activity

According to NSF (2004), Korea's performance in U.S. patent applications has been significant, especially since 1996. Samsung Electronics, a Korean company, ranked fifth among companies receiving U.S. patents in 2001. Also, Korea is the second-largest buyer of U.S. intellectual property next to Japan.[27] In 2001, Japan and Korea paid

---

[26] Technology Review and CHI Research, *The TR Patent Scorecard 2004*, www.technologyreview.com/scorecards/index.asp, accessed 31 October 2004.

[27] NSF (2004).

38.7 percent and 15.3 percent, respectively, of total U.S. receipts of royalties and fees.

Twelve Korean companies were listed in the TR Scoreboard of 2004. Five of them were ranked in the top 20 technologically strong companies in each technology category. All five are in electronics and semiconductors.

As Table 3.10 shows, Samsung Electronics and Samsung Group ranked 4th and 6th in semiconductors and electronics, respectively. Hynix ranked 13th in semiconductors, LG ranked 14th in electronics, and LG Philips ranked 18th. These statistics reflect the fact that Korea has only a few true global innovators in the country and they are basically concentrated in semiconductors and electronics. There were no Korean companies in the field of aerospace, biotechnology, pharmaceuticals, and computers in the TR Scoreboard.

Definitions of the indicators in the Table 3.10 are as follows:[28] "Technological strength" was calculated by multiplying the number of a company's U.S. patents by its current-impact index, which shows relative citation frequency (some patents cite scientific papers as prior art). "Science linkage" measures the average number of scientific references listed in a company's U.S. patents. A high figure indicates a company closer to the cutting edge than a company with a lower value. "Technology cycle time" indicates a firm's speed in turning leading-edge technology into intellectual property (IP). It is defined as the median age in years of the U.S. patents cited as prior art in the company's patents.

At the company level, in 2002 Samsung Electronics was the second-largest seller (5.5 percent of the market) in the semiconductor market after Intel (16.2 percent).[29] Samsung Electronics takes the largest share of the dynamic random access memory (DRAM) mar-

---

[28] Technology Review and CHI Research (2004).

[29] Bank of Korea (2003).

Table 3.10
Technological Strength of Selected Companies, 2003

	Tech Strength Rank	Company	Country	Number of U.S. Patents	Science Linkage	Technology Cycle Time
Semiconductors	1	Micron Technology, Inc.	United States	1,712	2.39	6.6
	2	Intel Corp.	United States	1,608	1.01	5.3
	3	Advanced Micro Devices, Inc.	United States	908	0.65	4.4
	4	Samsung Electronics	Korea	1,363	0.25	5.3
	13	Hynix Semiconductors, Inc.	Korea	448	0.40	5.0
Electronics	1	Hitachi Ltd.	Japan	2,189	0.55	6.5
	2	Matsushita Electric Industrial	Japan	1,944	0.46	6.0
	3	Canon, Inc.	Japan	2,061	0.64	7.1
	6	Samsung Group	Korea	1,577	0.25	5.3
	14	LG Electronics	Korea	465	0.15	5.2
	18	LG Philips LCD Co., Ltd.	Korea	227	1.01	5.3

SOURCE: Technology Review and CHI Research (2004).

ket. And Korean companies have the third-largest share of the SoC (System on a Chip) market, according to the Korea Ministry of Information and Communication.

As of 2002, the United States had 50.6 percent of the semiconductor market, followed by Japan with 26.4 percent and Europe with 11.3 percent. Korea had a 7.0 percent share of the semiconductor market. Korean semiconductor companies are basically focusing on DRAM, where Korea has the largest market share of 45.0 percent. In DRAM, the United States has 18.8 percent, Taiwan takes 13.1 percent, Europe has 11.7 percent, and Japan has 9.8 percent.

Even though Korea is expanding its share of the DRAM market, its share of the world's semiconductor export market is decreasing. This is because the demand for DRAM is growing more slowly than the demand for other types of semiconductors. DRAM demand is actually shrinking as the personal computer market becomes saturated. The DRAM market is heavily dependent on the PC market.

The Increase in China's High-Tech Exports Is Mainly Due to Foreign-Invested Companies

China's exports of high-technology products[30] increased at the extremely high rate of 33 percent per annum between 1997 and 2002 (Table 3.3)—reaching $67.9 billion, or 20.8 percent of its total exports in 2002. Although this performance is impressive, statistics show that foreign companies were the main contributors to the rapid increase.

Chinese companies focus on the assembly of high-tech products for export. Statistics on high-tech exports by trade mode reveal that almost 90 percent of the export products were either processed with imported materials (73.6 percent in 2001) or processed with supplied materials (15.6 percent in 2001). This suggests that the Chinese en-

---

[30] OECD defines high-tech industries as aircraft and aerospace, office and computing equipment, communications equipment, drugs and medicines, scientific instruments, and electrical machinery. See www.nsf.gov/sbe/srs/sei_nd93/chap6/doc/6s193.htm, accessed 14 December 2004.

terprises provided value-added in manufacturing or assembling processes while key technologies were outside China. The core materials were imported or supplied by foreign companies.

Export statistics by ownership also indicate a similar trend. In 2001, state-owned enterprises contributed to only 16.1 percent of total high-technology imports whereas foreign invested businesses, China-foreign joint ventures and Chinese cooperatives recorded respective shares of 48.2 percent, 30.2 percent, and 3.2 percent. Foreign invested businesses and China-foreign joint capital ventures

Table 3.11
High-Technology Exports by Trade Mode, 2000–2001 (US $billions)

Trade Mode	2000 Amount	2000 Composition	2001 Amount	2001 Composition
General trade[a]	3.27	8.8%	3.65	7.9%
Processing with supplied materials[b]	6.54	17.7%	7.26	15.6%
Processing with imported materials[c]	26.26	70.9%	34.21	73.6%
Leasehold trade[d]	0.07	0.2%	0.00	0.0%
Other[e]	0.90	2.4%	1.34	2.9%
Total	37.04	100.0%	46.45	100.0%

SOURCE: CMOST (2003c).

[a] Unilateral import or export trade by domestic businesses that have import and export permit.

[b] Foreign businessmen provide full or partial raw materials, auxiliary materials, components and parts, packaging material, and even equipment when necessary, and the Chinese party works on the processing or assembly according to the requirements of the other party. The finished goods are delivered to the foreign party for sale and the Chinese party collects the processing fees. If the foreign party provides equipment, the Chinese party makes up for the equipment costs by providing labor force.

[c] The Chinese party imports raw materials, materials, auxiliary materials, components and parts and packaging materials with foreign exchange and processes them into finished goods or semifinished goods for export.

[d] Import or export of goods under international lease contracts between the businesses who operate the lease and foreign businessmen.

[e] Includes equipment and goods for foreign equity investment, such as machinery, equipment, components, and other materials purchased by the foreign investor as his or her equity investment. Under the same category are also the transport tools, vehicles for production purpose and office equipment in a reasonable quantity for enterprises' own use, as defined by relevant state regulations.

remained the major players in China's high-tech exports in 2001, contributing to 78.4 percent of total exports.

Limited R&D Capability with Increasing Potential

In summary, S&T input and output indicators show that China has made significant progress in terms of growth on all indices, amount of highly educated R&D personnel, and number of science paper publications. However, it also faces significant challenges because of scarce investment resources and relatively low invention and innovation capability.

In nominal terms, China invests 10 percent more in S&T than Korea does, but the amount could be much larger in terms of purchasing power. China's investment in basic research is 1.3 times that of Korea, but it produces more than twice as many scientific papers as Korea. However, China's innovation capability in the indigenous industrial sector is still weak, and the country's R&D intensity is still low at 1.2 percent (2002).

China's R&D capability is concentrated in sectors other than industry, such as universities, research institutions, and government laboratories, which may not effectively respond to market incentives even though the Chinese government has tried to induce such an incentive shift. Thus, China may be less active in market-driven IP activities for some time to come.

CHAPTER FOUR
China's National Innovation System and R&D Strategies

In this chapter, we analyze the factors that may influence China's future S&T capacity and progress. They include the government's strategic policies and plans, its resource allocation emphasis, the efforts of the business sector, the contribution of foreign investors and foreign companies, the globalization of Chinese companies, and their acquisition of foreign companies.

We use a theoretical framework of the national innovation system (NIS) to analyze the structure and motivation underlying China's S&T capabilities in comparison with Korea's. In particular, the analysis focuses on basic science and generic technology capacity building, the role of universities as research units and suppliers of high-quality human resources, the governance of the national innovation system, the strategic emphasis of China's R&D programs, the roles and interactions of various R&D performers, and the strengths and weaknesses of the national innovation system.

China's National S&T Strategy

To understand China's S&T capabilities and its future potential, it is imperative to understand its underlying and stated national goals and objectives. China's S&T capabilities are built on and enhanced by the implementation of national strategies, policies, and plans. These are implemented through complex institutional arrangements and various R&D projects, augmented by the development of S&T human stock and boosted by foreign direct investment (FDI) inflows and outflows, as well as by international cooperation and exchange.

China's Core Development Strategy: "Rejuvenating the Nation Through Science and Education"

China has made S&T the cornerstone of its national economic progress since the early 1980s when its late leader Deng Xiaoping declared that "science and technology is the primary productive force" in China's economic development. In 1995, the importance of S&T was strengthened and further articulated as "rejuvenating the nation through science and education" in the "Joint Decision by the Central Committee of the Chinese Communist Party and the State Council on Accelerating Scientific and Technological Progress," which is regarded as the backbone of China's S&T strategy.

The adoption and implementation of the Joint Decision brought about significant reforms in China's national innovation system and rapid increases in R&D funding.[1]

- *Major Reforms in the S&T system.* Introduction of market mechanisms to make S&T better serve the needs of economic development; introduction of a national innovation system
- *Major Reforms in the education system.* Implementation of the "211 Project," streamlining and merging higher education institutions to establish 100 strong "Key Universities"
- *Significant increase in funding* for both S&T and education to kick-start the growth and progress of the reformed S&T and education systems
- *Construction and improvement in R&D infrastructure* by establishing National Key Laboratories (NKLs) and National Engineering Centers (NECs).

As a result of the reforms and measures taken, China's capabilities in S&T and education have been enhanced significantly, as

---

[1] See IDRC (1997), Suttmeier and Cao (1999), and OECD (2002a).

shown, in part, by the rapid increase in China's S&T output indicators.

S&T and Education Are the Two Pillars of China's Economic Development

In 2002, the Chinese government set an ambitious long-term goal to quadruple its GDP to US $4 trillion with a per capita GDP of $3,000 by the year 2020. The government plans to achieve this goal by "taking a new road to industrialization by implementing the strategy of rejuvenating the nation through science and education and that of sustainable development."[2]

Jiang Zhemin's Report to the 16th CPC Party Congress in 2002 set out the guidelines to implement the strategy of "rejuvenating the national through science and education" as follows:

- Pay close attention to improving the quality and efficiency of economic growth by relying on S&T and enhancing the quality of labor force.
- Strengthen basic research and high-tech research and promote innovations in key technologies and system integration so that China's S&T can develop by large strides.
- Acquire independent intellectual property rights in key areas on the frontiers of S&T.
- Deepen the reform on the administrative systems of S&T and education.
- Integrate S&T and education with the economy and expedite the pace of transforming research achievements into practical productive forces.
- Press ahead with building the national innovation system.

---

2 "Full text of Jiang Zemin's report at 16th Party Congress," 8 Nov. 2002, *People's Daily*, online at http://app1.chinadaily.com.cn/highlights/party16/news/1118full.htm, accessed 10 August 2004.

- Let venture capital function correctly to direct capital and human resources to start-ups and S&T innovation.[3]
- Improve the system of intellectual property rights protection.

Jiang Zhemin's report emphasizes that China's economic development is not to be isolated. China should be increasingly open to the outside world in order to "actively participate in international economic and technological cooperation as well as competition."

From the strategy and the guidelines above, we clearly observe the importance of the openness strategy to China and that S&T progress and education are two main pillars of future economic prosperity.

In Figure 4.1, we illustrate China's strategies and its vision of how these two pillars can be integrated into a "virtuous circle of development." Education contributes to higher productivity and advancement in S&T by providing high-quality R&D personnel. Education also promotes the efficiency aspect of the NIS, as well as economic development through higher income and consumption of well-educated workers. A vibrant NIS leads to advancement in various industrial technologies that can in turn promote economic development. Better economic development in turn can provide more resources to the development of education and S&T and the virtuous circle become self-reinforcing. The role of capital markets and the business sector is not yet in this picture. They will be introduced later in this chapter.

China's openness to the outside world has been a crucial contributor to its economic prosperity. Massive inflow of FDI greatly benefited China's economic development and enhanced its S&T capabilities and the quality of education and training. How well this strategy of openness has paid off and the role of the foreign sector in China will be discussed later.

---

[3] It is interesting that the role of venture capital is recognized in Jiang's report, whereas the role of the industrial sector is not emphasized. Probably this reflects the fact that China's economic development is planned and led by the government rather than industry.

Figure 4.1
China's Economic Development Strategy

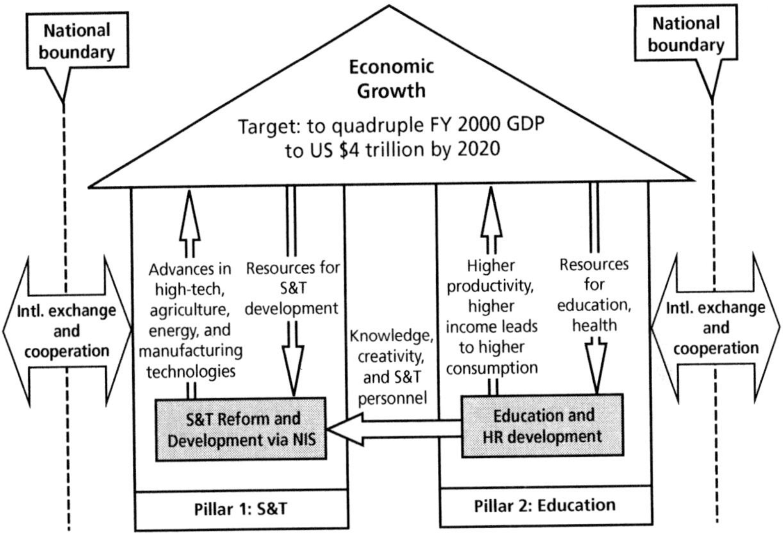

RAND MG320-4.1

China's National Innovation System

China started to explore the NIS concept in the early 1990s. In 1999, during the National Conference on Technology Innovation, the Chinese government announced that building and improving China's NIS was to be an important strategic task for the government.[4] Subsequently, the Chinese government has adopted the NIS as a systematic approach in implementing its national strategy of "rejuvenating China through science and education and sustainable development," as we saw in Jiang Zhemin's report of 2002.

---

[4] Jiang Zhemin's speech on "National Conference on Technology Innovation," 23 August 1999, (in Chinese), online at www.ccyl.org.cn/lkxjs/19990823.htm, accessed 23 September 2004.

Main Actors and Institutional Arrangement of the Chinese NIS

The main R&D performers of China's NIS are universities, R&D institutions, and enterprises. Figure 4.2 depicts the main actors and the interactions among them and other institutional arrangements in China's national innovation system. Below, we discuss the role of each actor and the institutional arrangements.

The Key Universities and the Chinese Academy of Science Are Major Knowledge Creators

R&D institutions are mainly government-owned and are represented by the Chinese Academy of Sciences (CAS). As of 2003, CAS operated 89 scientific research institutes with more than 20 supporting units, one university, and two graduate schools. These institutes are distributed over various parts of China.

Chinese universities, especially the 100 Key Universities, are a major force in education as well as R&D. The 100 Key Universities account for 72 percent of all Chinese university R&D expenditures and a large portion of all the students enrolled in higher education between 1995 and 2000.[5] The Key Universities and CAS are supposed to be the main repositories for knowledge creation in China.

The National Key Laboratories (NKLs) function as the basic research infrastructure and the National Engineering Centers (NECs) as a vehicle to facilitate technology transfer to industry and the assimilation of imported technologies. NKLs are usually established in the CAS or universities.

The industrial sector is not a strong knowledge creator yet in China. Chinese companies consumed 62 percent of China's gross R&D expenditures whereas they contributed 57 percent of total national R&D funding in 2002. However, as we saw in Chapter Three,

---

[5] CMOE, "Laying the Foundation for Rejuvenating the Nation Through Science and Education—A Summary of the Achievements of the 211 Project During the 9th Five-Year Plan Period," online at www.moe.gov.cn/edoas/website18/info5608.htm, accessed 19 October 2004.

Figure 4.2
The Main Actors and Linkages in China's NIS

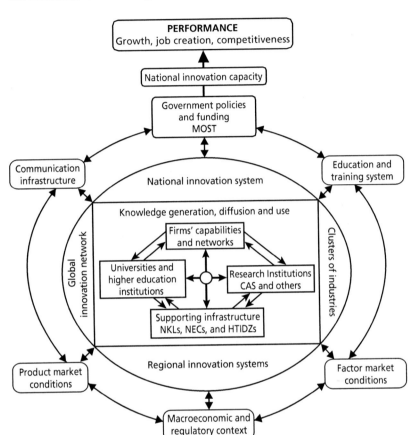

SOURCE: Adapted from OECD (1999).
RAND MG320-4.2

the Chinese industrial sector, in general, spends more resources on design activities than on invention and relies on external sources of technology more than on its own innovations and inventions. In terms of innovation capability, industry is one of the weak links in the Chinese NIS.

The CAS As a Reformed Research Powerhouse

The Chinese Academy of Science is a prestigious and influential research and development center in natural science, technological science, and high-tech innovation in China. Founded in 1949, it is supposed to be an equivalent of the U.S. National Academy of Sciences or the United Kingdom's Royal Society. However, unlike the National Academy of Sciences and the Royal Society, CAS operates its own research institutes. which function as the research arm of the government.

Between 1999 and 2000, CAS implemented an extensive reform called the Knowledge Innovation Program (KIP) to readjust its research focus and to restructure the organization. Management of research institutes was streamlined; many obsolete disciplines and research fields were discarded; some research institutes were transformed into enterprises or independent legal entities; and the practice of lifelong tenure was discarded.[6]

As of 2003, CAS has a total staff of over 44,000 in the research institutes and supporting institutes, approximately 30,000 of whom were research personnel and 5,000 administrative staff.[7] CAS researchers are the brightest scientists and engineers in China—in 2002, 5,000 had PhDs, 5,100 had MScs, and 6,700 had BScs. CAS's total income was RMB 10.04 billion (US $1.21 billion) in 2003. Chinese government funding accounted for 52 percent of CAS income; the other 48 percent came from nongovernmental sources.

With its intellectual power and facilities, CAS is a major force in R&D. In 2003, CAS was responsible for six (23 percent) out of 26 newly commissioned national basic research programs. Of 333 national key basic research projects, CAS was responsible for 92, accounting for 27.6 percent of the total. In the same year, 58 out of 160 national prominent young researchers (36 percent of the total) were CAS researchers. CAS took the lion's share of National Natural

---

[6] See "Progress in the Initial Phase of the KIP Pilot Project," online at http://english.cas.ac.cn/english/news/detailnewsb.asp?InfoNo=20964, accessed 25 September 2004.

[7] See CAS Annual Report 2003 (in Chinese), online at www.cas.cn/html/Books/O6121/b1/2003/index.htm#6.

Science Foundation (NSFC) funding for key projects, 46 percent in the year.[8]

CAS also serves as a major institute of graduate education. In 2002, it had 22,497 registered graduate students, of whom 9,736 were PhD candidates and 12,761 were MSc students. In the same year, it awarded 1,451 PhD degrees and 1,558 MSc degrees.

Recently, CAS has achieved some major high-tech break-throughs.[9] For example, it was able to build a "Dawning 3000" Super Server that has since become a main competitor to foreign products. CAS also completed sequencing and mapping the rice genome, a breakthrough widely acknowledged internationally. It is also known as a strong performer of R&D in carbon nanotubes and other new materials. In terms of SCI catalogued papers, the number of publication by CAS equaled the total number of papers from China's top 20 universities. The patents filed by CAS also increased dramatically. About 60 percent of the filed patents were classified as invention type, which is the highest percentage of all institutions in China.

CAS and its academic divisions are the highest advisory bodies in China concerning national S&T policy and development issues and have great influence on S&T policy issues.[10] For example, the 863 High-Tech R&D Program was initiated in 1986 at the suggestion of CAS Fellows.

CAS also maintains active interactions with the industrial sector. By the end of 2003, CAS had invested in 336 firms, 158 of which were under the full control of CAS (i.e., CAS held more than a 50 percent share of the companies).[11] Perhaps one of the most famous

---

[8] CAS annual report 2003.

[9] See "Progress in the Initial Phase of the KIP Pilot Project," online at http://english.cas.ac.cn/english/news/detailnewsb.asp?InfoNo=20964, accessed 25 September 2004.

[10] In 2004, there were 646 CAS Academicians (Fellows), of whom 41 were famous foreign scientists. CAS elects new Academicians on biannual basis. Academicians are elected from more than one million scientists and engineers in China and are considered the most respected scientists and researchers in their fields.

[11] See the CAS 2003 report on firms it has invested in, online at http://chanye.cashq.ac.cn/1.doc.

spin-offs from CAS is Lenovo Group (the former Legend Group). Legend started in 1984 with an investment of RMB 200,000 from CAS and has grown into a major force in China's computer industry.

The strong position of China's research institutes is reflected in the distribution of researchers over different institutions. As of 2002, almost 20 percent of the total number of scientists and engineers in China were with research institutes (See Table 4.1).

Table 4.1 Distribution of Scientists and Engineers by Sector (thousands of FTEs)

Sector	China, 2001 (%)	Korea, 2002 (%)
Higher education	167.6 (22.6%)	25.0 (17.6%)
Research institutes	147.7 (19.9%)	12.8 (9.0%)
Industry	388.5 (52.3%)	104.2 (73.4%)
Other	38.9 (5.2%)	—
Total	742.7 (100.0%)	141.9 (100.0%)

SOURCE: CMOST (2003c), KMOST (2004).

Universities As Major R&D Performers

Universities are the major research players and breeders of highly educated scientists and engineers. Chinese universities accounted for 77 percent of all international publication of science and engineering papers by Chinese in 2002, whereas government R&D institutions were responsible for 21 percent, leaving only 2 percent to enterprises and others.

In particular, the role of the 100 Key Universities is outstanding. The Key Universities were selected through the educational reform program called the "211 Project." The number 211 stands for 21st century, and 100 means that China plans to "reinvigorate the education system" by building 100 Key Universities and selecting a group of key subjects to meet the challenge of the 21st century. This initiative was a vehicle for government reform of the education system. At the same time, the government invested a significant amount of funds in the Key Universities on a scale "never seen in China's education history,"[12] thereby channeling allocations of state funds to more productive universities. This is another example of the Chinese government's strategy, called "focusing on doing something successfully while forgoing the others."[13]

The 211 Project was included in the 9th Five-Year Social Economic Development Plan (1995–2000), and its implementation started promptly in 1995. By the end of 2003, 98 universities and 602 key subjects had been included in the 211 Project. The Chinese government spent RMB 15 billion (US $1.81 billion) for this project between 1995 and 2000.[14]

Many universities were merged to pull resources together during the process. Science, technology, and engineering—including medicine, environment, resources, and agriculture—accounted for 80 percent of the 602 key subjects.

Although the number of universities included in the 211 Project is less than 10 percent of all the universities in China, the indicators in Table 4.2 show that the 100 Key Universities play a significant role in R&D, education, and training for S&T personnel. According to the China Ministry of Education, the Key Universities account for 72 percent of all Chinese universities' R&D expenditure.

The significant increase in funding resulted in dramatic improvements in the selected Key Universities. Between 1995 and 2000, the number of enrolled undergraduates, MSc candidates, and PhD candidates increased by 61 percent, 108 percent, and 101 percent respectively. R&D expenditure increased by 106 percent; the expenditure on R&D equipment increase by 98 percent; and the number of papers catalogued by SCI, EI, and ISTP increased by 94 percent. The top 100 Key Universities are expected to be a major force of China's

---

[12] CMOE, "Laying the Foundation for Rejuvenating the Nation Through Science And Education," www.moe.gov.cn/edoas/website18/info5608.htm, accessed 19 October 2004.

[13] This is a slogan that frequently appears in Chinese S&T policies. For example, see "The 10th Five-Year Science and Technology Development Plan," online at the Web site of CMOST: http://gh.most.gov.cn/zcq/ShowContent.jsp?db=KJGHLSQK&id=11, accessed 30 September 2004.

[14] CMOE (2004), ibid.

Table 4.2
Importance of 100 Key Universities in Research, Education, and Training in China, 1995–2000

Indicators	% Share of All Universities
Registered (enrolled) undergraduates	32
Registered MSc students	69
Registered PhD students	84
Instructors with PhD degrees	87
R&D expenditure	72
Costs of R&D equipments	54
State Key Laboratories	96

SOURCE: CMOE, www.moe.gov.cn/edoas/website18/ info5608.htm, accessed 19 October 2004.

R&D, especially in basic sciences, and they will play an important role in nurturing a large number of scientists and engineers in the future.

Chinese universities are not only a major force in basic research and nurturing scientists and engineers but also a strong R&D base for applied research and commercialization. By the end of 2002, 105 National Key Laboratories (i.e., more than two-thirds of the total Key Labs), 43 National Engineering Centers, 22 science and technology parks, and six technology transfer centers were affiliated with Chinese universities.

In recent years, universities in China have become hotbeds for high-tech spin-offs, so-called enterprises established by higher education institutions (EEHEIs).[15] CMOST statistics show that there were at least 4,389 EEHEIs related to 609 universities and colleges as of 2003. Total revenue of the EEHEIs is about RMB 82.7 billion (US $10 billion) and S&T-type EEHEIs accounted for 81 percent of the total revenue.

---

[15] EEHEIs were originally established or sponsored by universities. Universities have a major stake in these firms either as shareholders or supporters.

Beijing University and Tsinghua University are especially prominent in breeding successful EEHEIs. In 2003, Beijing Founder Group, affiliated with Beijing University, accounted for 19 percent of total sales of EEHEIs nationwide, while the three EEHEIs affiliated with Tsinghua University—Tongfang, Zhiguang, and Chengzhi—accounted for nearly 14 percent of total sales of EEHEIs.

Beijing Founder Group. Beijing Founder Group was established by Beijing University in 1986 to commercialize high-tech R&D results developed by Beijing University, initially focusing on Chinese electronic publishing technologies. In 1995, as a controlling shareholder, Beijing University restructured Beijing Founder into a holding company called Beijing Founder Group Corporation, injected its main assets into Founder Holdings Limited, and listed the Founder Holdings on the Hong Kong stock exchange.

In 2003, Beijing Founder Group achieved total sales of RMB 16.1 billion (US $1.95 billion). As of October 2004, Founder Group Co. controlled six listed companies in the stock exchanges of Shanghai, Shenzhen, Malaysia, and Hong Kong and had more than 20 wholly owned or joint venture companies. It had more than 15,000 employees. Founder Group is also one of the first six national technology innovation trial enterprises in China and is ranked among the top 500 large-scale state-owned companies in China.[16]

The Hong Kong listed company under Founder Group Co., Founder Holdings Ltd., achieved a turnover of HK $1,554 million (US $199 million, or more than one-tenth of the group's turnover) in 2003. As of December 31, 2003, it had 2,080 employees. The company is highly successful in software development and systems integration for the electronic publishing industry in Chinese and had secured a leadership position in China (90 percent market share) and in the overseas Chinese printing industry (80 percent market share). It is also a leading player in systems integration for the financial industry in China.

---

[16] See "Introduction to the Founder Group" (in Chinese) from the Founder Web site: www.founderpku.com/ljfz/jtjs.htm, accessed 20 October 2004.

Tsinghua Tongfang Co. Ltd. Tsinghua Tongfang Co. Ltd. (THTF) is an affiliated company of Tsinghua University and controlled by Tsinghua Holdings Ltd. It is another example of successful commercialization of R&D results from a university. During its initial growth period, THTF benefited greatly from Tsinghua University's participation in China's national Key Technology R&D Program. In 1991, Tsinghua University undertook a project entitled "research in detection systems for large-scale containers" and completed the project in 1995. The result was a successful and effective pilot detection apparatus for containers. This success enabled China to become one of the few countries in the world that produce such machinery, after the United Kingdom, France, and Germany.

THTF was listed on the Shanghai Stock Exchange in June 1997. It achieved an annual sales of RMB 6.8 billion (US $819 million) in 2003. The company has four core business sectors: IT, energy and environment protection, civilian application of nuclear technology, and fine chemicals and biomedicine. In IT, it focuses and has proprietary IP in information, computer, and digital TV systems. It is also a solutions provider for e-government, broadband communications, and digital media.

The Chinese Indigenous Industrial Sector Is a Relatively Weak Link in the NIS

The fact that China's major R&D capability is concentrated in sectors other than industry may slow down China's growth in innovation capability. The reason is that industry responds to market incentives more effectively than universities and government research institutes.

While Chinese universities and research institutes outperform their scarce investment in basic and applied research, the R&D performance of the Chinese industrial sector is not as impressive. Although Chinese enterprises accounted for 57 percent of R&D funding and 62 percent of national R&D expenditure in 2002, their share of industrial R&D in China's GERD is still low compared with other OECD countries. In part, this reflects the relatively large amount of nonprivate R&D activities and funding. Before 1999, industry accounted for less than 50 percent of R&D expenditure.

In general, the Chinese industrial sector lacks strong innovation capabilities and is heavily reliant on foreign technology. As we observed in the country-level patent analysis in Chapter Three, company-level statistics also confirms this fact.

The top ten electronic and IT companies in China filed an average of only 97 patents per year each between 1997 and 2001. This is not surprising if we look at the low R&D intensity of Chinese companies and the composition of industrial R&D by activity type in China.

According to OECD (2001), the R&D-to-sales ratio of the Chinese industrial sector was 1.0 percent whereas the ratio for electronic and communication industry, the most R&D intensive sector in China, was 1.99 percent. These figures are quite low compared to those in Korea. For the same year, Korea's R&D intensity for the whole of industry was 2.30 percent and that for communication equipment was 4.81 percent.[17]

Chinese companies spent over 92 percent of their R&D expenditure on development activities and less than 8 percent on basic and applied research (Table 4.3). According to OECD (2001), companies in OECD countries, including Korea, usually spend 60–77 percent of their R&D on development activities and 27–40 percent on basic and applied research.

Considering the record-breaking economic growth in China, it was probably a better strategy for Chinese companies to adopt readily available technologies instead of innovating on their own, which takes much more time than purchasing the technology.[18] In fact, we saw the same phenomenon in Korea at an earlier stage of development.

---

[17] Korea Industrial Technology Association (2004).

[18] Not surprisingly, Chinese companies spend more on importing technology than on their own R&D.

Table 4.3
Composition of Industrial R&D by Activity Type: International Comparison, 2000 (%)

	China	Korea	United States	Japan	United Kingdom	France	Australia
Basic research	0.4	6.1	8.0	5.8	4.8	4.5	3.3
Applied research	7.1	21.7	19.0	20.5	34.3	29.3	19.3
Experimental development	92.5	72.2	73.0	73.7	60.9	66.1	77.4

SOURCE: OECD (2001), CMOST (2003c).
NOTE: Japan and France data are for 1999; Australia, 1998.

However, this situation could change rapidly in China. In recent years, China's top 100 electronic and IT companies have been more active in patenting activities.[19] By the end of 2003, Haier had filed for a total of 4,774 patents, and BOE had applied for 2,125 invention patents.[20] This is significant progress considering that China's top ten electronic and IT companies filed only 3,886 patent applications between 1997 and 2001. The speed of this change is phenomenal.

There are many salient high-tech companies in China that are highly innovative. For example, Huawei's great success in global marketing and technological progress has pointed the way to an optimistic future for the Chinese industrial sector. Huawei was established in 1988, specializing in communications equipment. It attracted global attention partly due to its intellectual property rights dispute with Cisco Systems, the world's largest maker of routers and switches that transmit data and directs Internet traffic[21]. In 2003, Huawei's sales

---

[19] "Analysis of China's Top 100 Electronic and IT Companies—2003," IT Top 100 Net, online at www.ittop100.gov.cn/detail?record=1&channelid=1273&presearchword=ID=123963&channelin=1271, accessed 25 September 2004.

[20] BOE is the company that took over Hynix Semiconductors' Hydis.

[21] After Huawei agreed to stop selling disputed routers and switches and to modify its products, Cisco dropped its lawsuit. So far, Huawei has not been a serious threat to Cisco because

amounted US $2.83 billion, and its R&D-to-sales ratio was 10.1 percent. According to Huawei, it has proprietary IPR on many of its products and is one of the most active companies in patent applications in China (85 percent of them were invention-type patents). The number of Huawei's patent application has been growing at more than 100 percent per year. By the end of June 2004, Huawei had submitted 4,628 patent applications in China and 641 patents under the Patent Cooperation Treaty (PCT).[22]

The top innovators of China are still small compared with other global companies in innovation and marketing competition (Figure 4.3). For example, Huawei's cumulative international patent applications (not approvals) numbered only 641. Samsung Electronics alone was granted 1,363 U.S. patents in 2003, and the average number of U.S. patents granted to Samsung Electronics per year between 1998 and 2002 was 1,504.[23] Huawei's R&D expenditure in 2003 was US $385 million, about 13 percent of Samsung Electronics' US $2.9 billion R&D investment in the same year.[24] Huawei's total sales amounted to about 11 percent of Samsung Electronics' in 2003.

In general, more R&D does not necessarily bring higher profits. However, in companies that basically sell technological contents rather than commodities themselves, profitability generally moves together with R&D intensity. Plotting the profitability and R&D-to-sales ratio for the ten IT companies portrayed in Figure 4.3 gives positive evidence for this hypothesis, as Figure 4.4 shows.

Even though Chinese high-tech companies have had many success stories and noteworthy achievements, they are not as big as the world's leading companies in terms of sales, R&D expenditure, and net profits (see Figure 4.2). In 2003, the total sales of the top 100

Huawei only serves the low-cost end of the market. For more details, see Einhorn and Burrows, "Huawei: Cisco's Rival Hangs Tough," *Business Week,* 19 January 2004.

[22] "About Huawei's Intellectual Property Rights," online at www.huawei.com. cn/about/zhishi.shtml (in Chinese), accessed 10 September 2004.

[23] Technology Review and CHI Research, *The TR Patent Scorecard 2004,* online at www.technologyreview.com/scorecards/index.asp, accessed 15 August 2004.

[24] Data from company Web sites of Samsung Electronics and Huawei.

Figure 4.3
Comparison of Chinese High-Tech Companies and Leading Companies in the World: Total Sales, R&D Expenditure, and Profitability

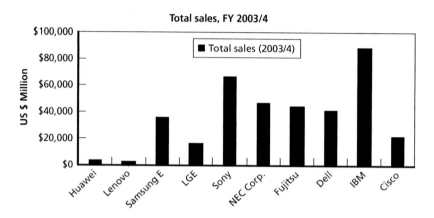

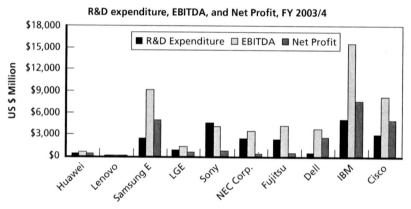

SOURCE: Annual reports of each company.
NOTE: Companies were selected because they are representative IT companies in each country. In terms of product portfolio, they are distributed over four different areas of business: Huawei and Cisco are in networking and communications equipment; Lenovo and Dell are PC and PC peripherals distribution; Samsung, LG, Sony are basically in consumer electronics; NEC, Fujitsu, and IBM are in corporate IT systems, software and components. Japanese companies may have low net profits for many reasons: a higher corporate tax rate, higher financial costs due to heavy dependency on borrowing, or a more diversified and integrated business structure. In terms of EBITA (Earnings Before Interest, Taxes, and Depreciation), Japanese companies' profits are higher but still not as high as those of IBM, Cisco, and Samsung.
RAND MG320-4.3

Figure 4.4
R&D Intensity and Profitability: Ten Global Companies in IT

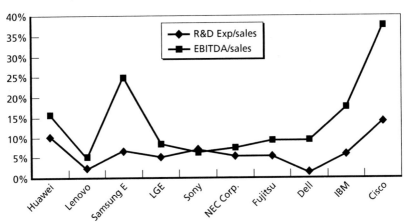

NOTE: Huawei's EBITDA/sales ratio is actually PBT/sales because not enough financial data are available (PBT = Profits before taxes).
RAND *MG320-4.4*

electronic and IT companies in China was US $82.7 billion,[25] which is only 2.2 times that of Samsung Electronics alone. The largest Chinese electronics company in terms of sales was Haier with US $9.7 billion, which is 27 percent of Samsung's sales.

China's large companies are basically in traditional industries. Sixteen Chinese companies were on the 2004 Fortune Global 500 list,[26] but none of them are in the high-tech industry. Without exception, all 16 of the Chinese companies on the Fortune 500 list were state-owned monopolies in the traditional industries of banking, insurance, energy, manufacturing, and utilities, including state power grid and telecom operators.

---

[25] "Analysis of China's Top 100 Electronics and IT Companies—2003."

[26] See www.fortune.com/fortune/global500, accessed 20 September 2004. The 16 Chinese companies on the Fortune 500 list are mainly state-owned monopolies in traditional industries such as banking, insurance, energy, manufacturing, and utilities companies (including state power grid and telecom operators).

Although China has made noteworthy progress in developing its high-tech capabilities in recent years, a majority of its high-tech companies are doing product assembly with core foreign technologies.[27]

The Chinese government expressed its concern about its relatively weak industrial R&D capability in the 10th five-year plan for high-tech industry:

> The innovation ability of the enterprises is weak and the problem of R&D being separated from enterprises has not been solved fundamentally. In addition, most enterprises have not become the main force in innovation. . . . There was little investment in commercializing R&D results and the rate of R&D results being successfully commercialized is very low.[28]

Recognizing this weakness in "demand pull" factors, in part inherited from China's tradition of government-led technology push in S&T development during the era of the Cold War and the communist economic system, the Chinese government has tended toward a strategy of entrusting most national R&D programs to R&D institutes and universities. The aim is to foster a flow of knowledge from the R&D institutions and universities to enterprises through such regional organizations as High Technology Industry Development Zones (HTIDZs) and science parks. According to a government survey of China's high-tech R&D program (the 863 Program), enterprise participation accounted for only about 30 percent of the total projects and 31 percent of the R&D expenditure of the program in 2002. Promoting regional NISs such as HTIDZs is a desirable strategy. However, the strategy of entrusting most national R&D programs to R&D institutes and universities may risk further weakening

---

[27] "China's Tech Ambitions Stuck on the Assembly Line," Reuters, 24 May 2004, online at http://www.usatoday.com/tech/world/2004-05-24-china-tech-lags_x.htm, accessed 17 September 2004.

[28] See "The 10th Five-Year High-Tech Development Plan" (in Chinese), available from CMOST's Web site: http://gh.most.gov.cn/zcq/ShowContent.jsp?db=KJGHSWZDZXGH&id=7, accessed 10 August 2004.

the link between R&D bodies and market incentives as well as the innovation capability of the enterprises.

China's S&T Policy Governance Structure

Even after the major market-oriented reforms in the past two decades, China's S&T management system is still highly centralized and hierarchical, with emphasis on central government planning, strict organizational procedures, and a unified policy framework.

Hierarchical and Centralized

S&T policy governance in China involves three hierarchical tiers: (1) a top decisionmaking body, (2) implementing and coordinating agencies, and (3) institutions that carry out the action plans, i.e., R&D institutions such as universities, research institutes, and enterprises.[29]

The highest-level government body responsible for decisionmaking in S&T and education policy is the State Council State Steering Committee of S&T and Education, headed by Premier Wen Jiabo.

The most important government institution in terms of national S&T policies and their implementations is the China Ministry of Science and Technology (CMOST).[30] CMOST has been given the responsibilities of managing and coordinating national S&T activities and resource allocation, while other governmental agencies are authorized to take the responsibilities for formulating and implementing corresponding policies or short-term projects.

---

[29] Chinese Embassy in New Zealand, "Overview of China's S&T Management System," online at www.chinaembassy.org.nz/eng/kj/t39433.htm, accessed 14 December 2004.

[30] For the main responsibilities and functions of CMOST, refer to the Web site of CMOST, www.most.gov.cn (in Chinese), and the Chinese Embassy in New Zealand, "Overview of China's S&T Management System," online at www.chinaembassy.org.nz/eng/kj/t39433. htm, accessed 14 December 2004.

Because of the centralized nature of S&T policy governance in China, CMOST is responsible for organizing, directing, and implementing all the national civilian S&T programs, such as key basic research projects (973 Program), the high technology R&D program (863 Program), the Torch Program, and many others to be discussed later in this chapter.

CMOST's mandates also include identifying priorities for China's future S&T development and formulating national medium- and long-term R&D. For example, between 2002 and 2003, CMOST conducted the "Foresight 2003" study to identify priorities for future development in China's high-tech R&D. The result of Foresight 2003 will be incorporated into the formal planning and priority setting process for China's S&T policy.[31]

The roles of other ministries and institutions in S&T policy are as follows: The China Ministry of Education (CMOE) monitors Chinese higher education institutions that are main actors of basic research and breeders of S&T human resources; the National Natural Science Foundation (NSFC) provides funding for about 60,000 researchers in basic research every year; and the Chinese Academy of Sciences (CAS) advises the government on S&T strategies and policies.[32]

The third tier consists of the institutions that carry out the action plans, such as universities, research institutes and enterprises.[33] The roles of these R&D performers have already been discussed in this chapter.

Comparison with Korea's New S&T Policy Governance

Korea's S&T policy governance is less hierarchical but quite similar to China's. The highest decisionmaking body is the National Science and Technology Council, headed by the President of Korea. In plan-

---

[31] The Foresight results will be introduced later in this chapter and also in Chapter Five.

[32] For the details of China's S&T policy governance, refer to Huang et al. (2004).

[33] "Overview of China's S&T Management System," online at www.chinaembassy. org.nz/eng/kj/t39433.htm, accessed 14 December 2004.

ning and implementing national S&T programs, the Korea Ministry of Science and Technology (KMOST) has so far not held an absolutely dominant position in terms of budget allocation and implementing S&T policies. KMOST accounted for about 20.6 percent of the government R&D budget in 2003.[34] KMOST is in a position somewhat parallel to that of the Ministry of Commerce, Industry, and Energy (MOCIE), which accounted for 20.3 percent of government R&D in the same year. A number of ministries each accounted for more than 10 percent of the total government R&D budget.[35]

However, in September 2004 the S&T policy governance structure of Korea became more centralized. KMOST was empowered to plan, evaluate, and coordinate major S&T policies and programs of all the ministries. KMOST is also in charge of allocating and coordinating national R&D resources among different ministries. In the process of changing its policy governance, the Korean government has drawn on the NIS concept and has emphasized the necessity of the system approach. The Korean government hopes that this new governance system will solve the ongoing problem of duplicative R&D projects initiated by different ministries and bring more efficient NIS in Korea.

China Promotes R&D in a Few Focused Areas

As articulated in the 10th Five-Year S&T Development Plan, the Chinese planners have opted for strategic allocation of resources in developing its S&T capabilities, called "focusing on doing something successfully while forgoing the others." Technologies chosen to be given priority will be supported intensively; the rest will get fewer resources.[36]

---

[34] KISTEP (2004), p. 70.

[35] Ibid.

[36] This strategy is not new. It was used in the late 1950s and 1960s when China was developing its first atomic and hydrogen bombs and its first satellite.

Next-Generation Emerging Technologies in China: IT, Biotechnology, and New Materials

China Technology Foresight 2003 identified key technologies that would be given priority in China's future national plans.[37] These technologies include the following: (1) ten sciences and technologies in which the experts believed that China could make important breakthroughs and produce important proprietary intellectual properties within the next five to ten years; (2) 21 national key technologies that will enhance China's international competitiveness and national security; (3) technologies in which China may realize leap-forward development in industrial application in the next ten years.

After studying international and domestic S&T development trends and taking China's future socioeconomic development into consideration, experts selected 222 topics that were believed either to be opportune for China or to have reasonable chances for China to develop in the next five to ten years.[38]

Foresight 2003 focused on three major technology areas: information technology, biotechnology, and new materials.

- *Information technology.* Next-generation mobile telecom (beyond 3G), 64-bit computer processing units (CPUs), next generation common software, nanometer grade technology and instruments for System-on-Chip (SoC), and digital audio/video technology.
- *Life sciences and biotechnology.* Functional genomics and proteomics, biomedical technology, biocatalysis and biotransformation, trans-gene breeding technology for new farm crops, industrial and environmental biotechnology, biosafety and biotech quality control, and tissue and organ engineering.
- *New materials.* Nanomaterials and nanotechnologies, high-performance metal structural material, microelectronics and optoelectronics, advanced composite materials, next-generation en-

---

[37] The Foresight results were published by CMOST in a report entitled "China Technology Foresight 2003."

[38] For the details of Foresight 2003, see Yang et al. (2004).

ergy materials, biomedical materials, and environmentally friendly materials and technologies.

The findings of Foresight 2003 will be significant inputs into the S&T development plans of the 11th Five-Year Plan (2006–2010) and also the Medium- to Long-Term Development Plan (MLDP) for Science and Technology (2006–2020). The above major areas will receive priority support from Chinese government. Because the formulation of MLDP is still in progress, there is little information on the final contents of the plan at present.

Comparison with Korea's Focus on Future Technologies

Foresight 2003 can be compared with Korea's choice of six high technologies (6T) as promising future technologies. The six areas include information technology (IT), biotechnology (BT), nanotechnology (NT), environmental technology (ET), aerospace technology (AT), and cultural technology (CT). The first three categories overlap with China's three focus areas; the other three areas also get significant support from the Korean government budget. Government R&D expenditure on 6T made up 30 percent of the total government R&D budget in 2004. Out of a budget of 1.8 trillion Korean won (about US $1.7 billion) for the 6T program, IT accounted for 7.8 percent, BT for 9.1 percent, NT for 3.6 percent, ET for 5.3 percent, ST for 3.7 percent, and CT for 0.4 percent.[39]

China's Major National R&D Programs

The major nondefense national programs under CMOST can be categorized into four main areas:

- *Basic research.* The 973 Program and other projects funded by NSFC

---

[39] KISTEP (2004), p. 16.

- *Applied R&D.* Strategic high-tech R&D (863 Program) and key technology R&D programs
- *Industrialization of R&D results and technology.* The Torch Program, Spark Program, and S&T-based Small- and Medium-Sized Enterprises (SMEs) technology innovation fund
- *R&D infrastructure-building.* National Key Laboratories for key R&D facilities and National Engineering Centers for technology transfer and assimilation.

Figure 4.5 illustrates the major national R&D programs and their goals in the framework of its NIS. The objectives, main charac-

Figure 4.5
China's Major S&T Programs in the Framework of the NIS

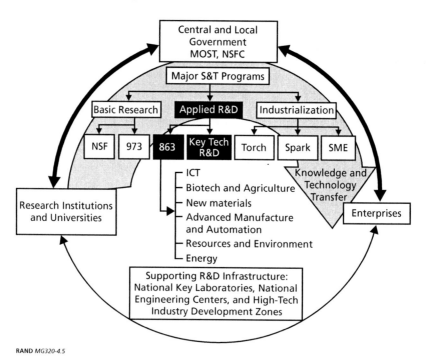

RAND *MG320-4.5*

teristics, and budget allocation of the programs are summarized in Appendix B.

Of these programs, the 973 Program, 863 Program, and Torch program deserve special attention because they are key to China's future S&T capability in high-tech R&D and industrialization.

The National Basic Research Program (973 Program)

The main areas and exemplary projects supported by the National Basic Research Program (973 Program) are as follows:[40]

- *Agriculture.* Trans-gene farm crops; biological nitrogen fixation
- *Energy.* Basic and fundamental research in oil, gas, coal, solar energy, hydrogen storage, fuel cells
- *Information.* Basic research on computing, optical information storage, integrated circuits (ICs), quantum communication and quantum devices
- *Resources and Environment.* Fundamental studies in mineral, oil, gas deposition, ecosystems
- *Biotechnology.* Basic research in health-related fields such as stem cells, reproductive system, diseases
- *Materials.* Nanomaterials and structures, superconductors, fundamental studies on alloys, advanced engineering materials
- *Synthesis and Frontier Science.* Frontiers of core mathematics, ultra-intense, ultra-short laser science, protein functions, crucial problems in nonlinear science, radioactive ion beam and nuclear astrophysics, high-energy radiation from space.

From the inception of the 973 Program in 1997 to the end of 2002, a total of RMB 2.5 billion (US $302 million) was spent on the program, with each project receiving an average of US $3–5 million over its five-year life cycle. In 2004, the Chinese government plans to

---

[40] See: "Profile of 973 Program," from the official 973 Program Web site at www.973. gov.cn/English/Index.aspx, accessed 12 October 2004.

spend RMB 0.9 billion (US $109 million) on the 973 Program.[41] Note that the budget allocation for the National Basic Research program is relatively small, as we saw from China's aggregate expenditure on basic research in Chapter Three.

The National High-Technology R&D Program (863 Program)

The 863 Program is China's strategic high-technology R&D program, designed (1) to pool the best technological resources in China for the purpose of keeping up with the world's high-tech advances in selected fields, (2) to close the gap between China and other countries and (3) to attempt to make breakthroughs in several critical areas.

The 863 Program is designed for both military R&D and civilian R&D, and its principles illuminate the Chinese government intention to make use of civilian R&D results for military use.[42]

The guiding principles for the 863 Program are as follows: setting limited targets, defining priorities, vigorously monitoring global technological advances, striving for breakthroughs wherever possible, and combining military and civilian R&D while focusing attention on civilian R&D.

The program concentrates its efforts in eight priority areas: (1) biotechnology and modern agriculture, (2) information, (3) advanced manufacturing and automation, (4) energy, (5) advanced materials, (6) resources and environment, (7) marine, (8) space and laser. The first six areas are deemed civilian R&D and are managed and implemented by CMOST as shown in Figure 4.5. The marine, space, and laser programs are run on a confidential basis.[43]

---

[41] "'The management of 863 Program will be more open and fair'"—interview with Ma Songde, Vice Minister of MOST," *Guangming Daily*, 30 August 2004, online at www.gmw.cn/01gmrb/2004-08/30/content_89716.htm (in Chinese).

[42] Defense experts have often argued that China makes substantial investments in science and technology with military applications and that civilian programs sometimes serve to hide what are actually military expenditures. In fact, in the early 1980s the Chinese government forced many military-related industries to produce manufactured goods for the civilian market.

[43] Hsiung (2002).

Reports on the 863 Program usually show civilian side expenditures, achievements, and future spending plans. Data for defense R&D under the 863 Program are not readily available. Between 2001 and 2005, China plans to spend RMB 15 billion (US $1.81 billion) in the six civilian R&D areas, almost 2.7 times that of the total spending in the 15 years between 1986 and 2001.[44] In 1986–2001, total expenditure of the 863 Program was 11 billion RMB ($1.33 billion);[45] the six civilian areas accounted for 5.7 billion RMB ($689 million),[46] about 52 percent of the total. From these figures, we can infer the military R&D of the 863 program between 1986 and 2001 was about 5.3 billion RMB ($641 million) and 48 percent of the 863 Program budget.[47]

One survey reported that, 15 years after the 863 Program commenced, China had remarkably narrowed its overall technology gaps with the advanced world.[48] Sixty percent of the technologies started from scratch had reached or approached an internationally comparable level; 11 percent had attained an internationally advanced level.[49]

One of the successes of the 863 Program is Datang's TD-SCDMA standard.[50] The involvement of Siemens AG was crucial for Datang Telecom Technology and Industry Group's ability to develop

---

[44] For a full review, see "863 Program Spurs Science and Technology," *Beijing Review* (2001), online at www.bjreview.com.cn/2001/CoverStory/FM200113a.htm, accessed 15 August 2004.

[45] "What Did the 863 Program Bring to the Chinese?" *China Youth Daily*, 27 February 2001, online at www.863.org.cn/863_95/medium/med016.html, accessed 15 September 2004.

[46] *Beijing Review* (2001).

[47] This figure should not be considered accurate. Because China has been secretive about defense R&D expenditure and also because the 863 Program has evolved and changed during the course of more than 18 years of operation, a simple combination of figures from nonofficial sources would produce quite limited information.

[48] *China Youth Daily*, 27 February 2001.

[49] This figure was not reported in *Beijing Review* but is available in Chinese from "Our Country's High-Tech Is Eye-Catching—11% Have Reached World Advanced Level," http://job.costind.gov.cn/company/artical/004.htm, accessed 23 October 2004.

[50] See www.863.org.cn/15year/industrial/index_inf.html (in Chinese).

the technology. Siemens AG spent more than $200 million since 1998 working with Datang to develop TD-SCDMA. Datang was a state-owned research institute under the Ministry of Information and Industry when it started collaborative research with Siemens. TD-SCDMA was approved by the International Telecommunication Union (ITU) as one of the three standards for third-generation (3G) mobile telecommunication technology. Siemens is to develop a 3G phone with Huawei based on this new standard TD-SCDMA. This 3G standard may have major repercussions within China and beyond, if China decides to use it as the national 3G standard.

The Torch Program

The Torch Program has been quite successful in building up China's increasing high-tech industrial base and it seems to have done well in industrializing some R&D results. It deserves more discussion because the rise of high-tech industries in China could have major repercussions for both China and Korea as well as for many of China's main trading partners.

The Torch Program aims to accelerate commercialization of R&D results and industrialization of high technology. Through the Torch Program, 53 High-Technology Industry Development Zones (HTIDZs) have been established.

HTIDZs were designed as clusters of universities, research institutes, and industries and they did successfully achieve a virtuous circle: The growing clusters invited more and more firms every year. For example, many Chinese high technology companies including Lenovo Group (former Legend Group) and Huawei are residents of the HTIDZs.[51] Research centers of foreign high-tech companies such as Microsoft, Motorola, IBM, Nokia, Samsung Electronics, and LG group are also residents of HTIDZs.

The growth of the HTIDZs has been nothing short of a miracle: Between 1992 and 2003, average annual growth rates of sales, export, and net profits were 51 percent, 55 percent, and 42 percent respec-

---

[51] Lenovo Group is the largest PC manufacturer in Asia excluding Japan.

tively. The high growth was mainly due to rapid growth in the number of firms coming into HTIDZs or newly established there. As of 2003, the HTIDZs accommodated 33,000 firms and 3.95 million employees. Total sales of companies in HTIDZs reached US $253 billion with US $51 billion in exports.[52]

With such rapid growth, the large volume of sales and exports, and the number of people being employed in HTIDZs, it is not hard to see why the HTIDZs have been hailed as a great success in contributing to rapid economic development at both the national and regional levels. However, their profits are not as impressive. In 2003, the average net profit-to-sales ratio of the HTIDZ companies was 5.4 percent, and average gross profit before tax to sales ratio was 10.1 percent.[53] This is not much higher than the before-tax gross profit rate of total manufacturing in China, which was 9.4 percent in 2001.[54]

The Torch Program also established various technology incubators and Productivity Promotion Centers (PPCs) to facilitate technology transfer, nurture high-tech-based companies and entrepreneurs, and provide training. *Technology incubators* are intermediaries that foster closer links between start-up companies and other NIS stakeholders, such as universities, R&D institutes, government bodies, financial institutions, and S&T personnel.

We can clearly see that the Chinese government aims to build clusters of industry and regional innovation systems based on the NIS framework shown in Figure 4.1 to promote the commercialization of R&D results and industrialization of high technologies. China's strong leverage of its large domestic market and abundant human resource contributed significantly to the success of this approach.

---

[52] S&T Statistics, "2003 Comprehensive Report on New and High-Tech Industry Development Zone," online at www.sts.org.cn/tjbg/gjscy/documents/2003/0809.htm (in Chinese), accessed 26 August 2004.

[53] Ibid.

[54] Authors' calculation from CMOST (2003c), p. 224.

Interaction with the Foreign Sector

Interaction with the foreign sector has been important for China's economic development and technological progress. As we have seen in the analysis above, foreign companies and foreign joint ventures play a major role in high-tech exports and invention patents. In addition, the foreign sector helped improve China's S&T capabilities through several different channels:

- Technology transfer
- Education and training
- Learning by doing through original equipment manufacturing or other joint ventures
- Exposure to modern management skills and production technology
- R&D cooperation among foreign companies, universities, and research institutes
- More competitive markets.

FDI Contributed Significantly to China's Economic Development

China has been one of the world's largest recipients of foreign direct investment in recent years, and it overtook the United States to become the largest recipient of FDI in 2003, with an inflow of US $53.5 billion.[55] Foreign direct investment in China has contributed significantly to China's rapid economic development. A study by the International Monetary Fund (IMF) showed that FDI in China contributed nearly 3 percent to China's annual GDP growth during the 1990s.[56] In other words, FDI explains almost a third of China's GDP growth rate, whereas its share of total fixed-asset investment averaged only 12.5 percent in average between 1993 and 2002.

FDI also provides many job opportunities for the Chinese: By the end of 2002, the number of employees in foreign invested enter-

---

[55] UNCTAD, "The World Investment Report 2004: The Shift Towards Services," September 2004, online at www.unctad.org/en/docs/wir2004_en.pdf, accessed 3 October 2004.

[56] Tseng and Zebregs (2002).

prises (FIEs) had reached 23.5 million, accounting for 11 percent of China's urban work force.[57] FIEs have conducted extensive training of a massive number of Chinese employees to enable them to use the FIEs' advanced technologies and to operate within their advanced management systems. According to Tung (2003), FIEs accounted for 33.4 percent of industrial output, 52.2 percent of total export, and 21 percent of tax revenue in 2002.

Interaction with the foreign sector has contributed significantly to the rise of high-tech industries in China. Chinese electronic and telecommunication equipment manufacturers such as Huawei, Zhongxing, TCL, and Haier are great examples that show how the massive inflow of FDI has enabled Chinese indigenous companies to compete seriously with incumbent foreign firms.[58]

Another example is the role of international venture capitalists in taking Chinese start-up firms to NASDAQ. Behind the NASDAQ initial public offerings (IPOs) of Chinese PC manufacturers such as UT Starcom, software companies such as Asiainfo, and Internet companies such as Sina, Netease, Sohu, and Ctrip were foreign venture capitalists investing in and nourishing Chinese start-ups. Ironically, Chinese government regulation of venture capital—prohibition of local funding or IPOs in China—contributed to the move by international venture capitalists toward IPOs on NASDAQ.

Education and Training by Foreign Invested Enterprises (FIEs)
FIEs can contribute to China's technological progress through several channels:[59]

- *Conducting joint R&D with Chinese researchers.* Because of the strong market orientation of foreign multinational corporations' R&D, this type of joint work has greatly enhanced the commer-

---

[57] Tung (2003).

[58] Tan (2002).

[59] Wang and Li (2004).

cial acumen of some high-level Chinese R&D personnel, in turn helping the commercialization of R&D results.

- *Management localization.* Some MNCs regularly send senior and mid-rank Chinese managers to headquarters to receive training and orientation. This helps to nurture modern management knowledge and skills in a large number of high-level Chinese managers. For example, the ratio of local Chinese in Motorola's management team in China was only 12 percent in 1994. By the end of 2000, the ratio had increased to 74 percent.

- *Providing multilevel training to local employees, including management, finance, sales and marketing, production, quality control, and human resources (HR) training.* Because the management of the Chinese operation must be integrated with that of headquarters, MNCs have to transfer the know-how in management to their Chinese operation.

- *Providing training services to local domestic companies.* For example, Motorola worked with the State Planning Commission to form an "Enterprise Optimization Center" and provided various of training methods and suitable rules and regulations to Chinese enterprises. By the end of 2001, Motorola had provided training to some 400 Chinese enterprises and trained some 1,400 high-level managers and technical personnel.

The high-level managers and technical personnel trained by FIEs are mobile. They often serve as a reserve of high-quality human resources that indigenous Chinese companies or new high-tech start-ups can draw on.

Technology Transfer from Foreign Sources: "Market for Technology"
Many case studies and empirical analyses show the benefit of technology transfer and diffusion by FIEs.[60] China's large market has been a lever of control for the Chinese government to expedite technology transfer from foreign companies in China. Adopting a "mar-

---

[60] See Cheung and Lin (2004), Hu, Jefferson and Qian (forthcoming), Fan (2002), Wang and Li (2004), Chen, Cheung, and Zhang (1995), Young and Lan (1997).

ket for technology" policy, the Chinese government has actively negotiated with foreign companies requesting technology transfer in return for opening its market to them.

Before China joined the WTO, the Chinese government used to encourage foreign firms to set up joint ventures with Chinese partners.[61] To set up the joint venture, the government established requirements ranging from a certain quota of locally produced parts to outright transfer of technology to the Chinese partners. The Chinese government wanted the local Chinese firms to learn and assimilate the foreign technologies and management techniques.

As long as Chinese partners have enough absorption capability, the "market for technology" strategy will be successful. The case of the Chinese power generation industry is a promising example.

In 2002, GE, Mitsubishi, and other foreign power equipment manufacturers were invited to bid on contracts to supply power turbines to China. Associated technology transfer was a requirement in the bid. GE won the bid[62] and agreed to a considerable amount of technology transfer to its Chinese partners, Harbin Power Equipment Company (HPEC) and Shenyang Liming Aero-Engine Group Corp. According to the *Wall Street Journal,* GE agreed to provide technical drawings of a key cooling system and the advanced metallurgy of the blades to allow the Shenyang venture to manufacture the second and third rows of blades inside the turbine.[63] GE also agreed to let Harbin Power Equipment Ltd., a state-owned power company, to assemble GE's turbines at its factory in Northeastern China.[64] Harbin will also manufacture most of the less sophisticated components in the turbine.

---

[61] Many foreign companies prefer to establish wholly-owned companies in China for the sake of IPR protection, among many reasons.

[62] "GE Power System Won US$900 Million Bid to Supply Turbines to China," www.ge-china.com/product/power/ge-power1.htm, (in Chinese), accessed 9 September 2004.

[63] Kranhold (2004).

[64] "GE Energy Signs Service Joint Venture Agreement in China," 1 March 2004, online at www.ge-china.com/genews/read.asp?newsid=591, accessed 9 September 2004.

It will take China some time to be able to fully exploit what it learns from foreign partners. However, this kind of deal will provide great opportunities for Chinese companies and employees to learn and progress in technological capability. Given the increased competition among foreign investors that want access to China's huge market, the Chinese government could drive the foreign investors to agree to transfer technologies to China.

R&D Centers of Foreign Multinational Corporations in China

China's market for technology extends to an active recruitment of foreign multinational corporation R&D laboratories. If foreign companies want to have manufacturing facilities in China, Chinese government officials encourage them to establish R&D centers and training centers. The China Ministry of Commerce believes that the government's strong support is one of the factors explaining the recent increase in R&D centers in China.[65]

Some experts assert that foreign companies establish R&D centers and training centers to put key officials in China at the initial period of investment as part of overall investment package to get tax and other benefits, but that they are not doing core R&D in China—probably because of China's poor IPR protection. Foreign R&D centers often work in such areas as usability of equipment and platform and local customer support.

From our interviews with R&D managers of foreign research laboratories in China, we found that the above assertion was only partly true. Of course, the core R&D activities are mainly done at headquarters. However, some lower-end R&D and China-specific R&D activities are operated within companies' Chinese laboratories.

Managers of many foreign R&D centers in China perceived opening R&D facilities in China as a way to tap into human resources in China. This was regarded as a productive way to handle a spectrum of labor-intensive R&D activities, because highly educated

---

[65] "R&D Centres Draw Firms Closer to Clients," *China Daily*, 17 August 2004, online at www.chinadaily.com.cn/english/doc/2004-08/17/content_366104.htm, accessed 30 August 2004.

and skilled people are needed and because local researchers can serve the local market better.

A recent global survey of senior executives by the Economist Intelligence Unit (2004) also confirms this positive attitude toward establishing R&D centers in China.[66] China ranked at the top for destination of overseas R&D spending in the next three years, followed by the United States, India, the UK, and Germany. The hunt for research talent, the size of the local market, and as cost considerations are the key drivers. According to the report, companies still prefer that high-end R&D be done in developed counties because IPR protection was a key concern for many senior executives. Developing countries, including China, are favored for lower end of the value chain, mainly for conducting product development. Nevertheless, China is moving up the ladder because it is identified as an important location for ground-breaking research in mobile technology.

According to a report from the China Ministry of Commerce, foreign investors have set up more than 600 R&D centers in China as of June 2004, mainly in the areas of telecommunications, electronics, automotive, pharmaceutical, and chemical industries. The foreign firms spent a total of US $4 billion to set up these centers. Most of them were set up in the past two years, with 400 being opened since 2002.

Setting Technology Standards: The Large Domestic Market As Leverage

The Chinese government has made setting China's own technical standards a post-WTO strategy because it aims to protect its own interests while working within the WTO framework. This strategy, along with its implementation, was clearly spelled out in a CMOST publication in 2002.[67]

---

[66] Economist Intelligence Unit (2004).

[67] "Chinese S&T Community Ready for WTO," *CMOST China Science and Technology Newsletter* (in English), Issue No. 283, 20 January 2002, online at www.most.gov.cn/English/newletter/Q283.htm, accessed 29 September 2004.

In 2003, China proposed its own wi-fi standard.[68] It was enthusiastically accepted in China but resisted by the world's major players. Although China finally caved in to the immense international pressure by agreeing to indefinitely postponing the enforcement of the standard in China, it shows what China could do if it wanted. China has such an enormous domestic market it could afford to "go it alone" if needs be.

China is promoting TD-SCDMA, one of the three ITU-approved standards for 3G mobile communication, as the standard for the next- generation cellular phone. This has gained considerable attention both in the United States and Europe. Many MNCs are now teaming with local firms to get ready for China's push for 3G mobile. As mentioned above, Siemens worked with Datang to develop TD-SCDMA but has teamed up with Huawei for 3G mobile equipment manufacturing.

China is also proposing its own digital video disc and players standard called EVD (enhanced versatile disc), which is expected to have four to five times the storage capacity of current DVD discs. In addition, China is actively supporting open-source computing to reduce its dependence on Microsoft Windows.

By setting its own standards, China aims to avoid steep royalty payments to patent-holding firms in Japan, the United States, and Europe. Some reports were showing that the Chinese manufacturers have to pay patent fees of some US $20 out of the sale of a US $60 DVD player, making the margin unbearably slim for Chinese manufacturers.[69]

---

[68] *Wi-fi* means wireless fidelity. The term is used generically when referring to any type of 802.11 network.

[69] "Chinese Enterprises Could Not Afford Large Amount of Patent Royalties and Have Stopped Exporting General DVD Players," *Guangzhou Daily,* 12 March 2004, online at http://tech.tom.com/1121/2048/2004312-86336.html, accessed 29 October 2004. A related article is "Data Showed That Manufacturers in Guangdong Province Can Only Make Profit of Approximately US $1 per DVD Player Sold" (in Chinese), *Sina S&T,* 10 August 2004, online at http://tech.sina.com.cn/it/2004-08-10/0821401236.shtml, accessed 28 October 2004.

Overseas M&A Activities by Chinese Companies

Not only is China a large recipient of FDI, but it has also become an increasingly important investor in other countries in recent years. According to UNCTAD (2003), during the 1990s, China's average annual FDI outflow was $2.3 billion, slightly lower than Korea's $2.9 billion.

China's recent outward FDI has concentrated mainly on access to natural resources and markets and the acquisition of such strategic assets as technology and brand names.

The Chinese government views the ability to compete globally as the key to cultivating its own transnational companies and it has been encouraging strong Chinese companies, mainly state-owned enterprises, to invest outside of China in its "going out" strategy. Such steps as simplifying the approval process, decentralizing the controls, and publishing overseas investment information were taken.[70] The Chinese EXIM bank has also pledged strong financial support to "going out" projects in industries such as shipbuilding, equipment, telecommunication, materials, energy, and power generation.[71]

The following two cases are examples of Chinese companies "going global" to secure markets and/or to acquire technology.

TCL-Thompson Electronics. On January 28, 2004, TCL Group, China's leading TV and consumer electronics maker, signed an agreement to merge its TV and DVD business with that of Thompson of France. The joint venture is called TCL-Thompson Electronics (TTE).

In 2003, before the merger, Thompson's TV and DVD business was reported to have lost 120 million euros in 2003, whereas TCL's TV unit gained a profit of RMB 530 million (US $64 million) do-

---

[70] "It Is Now Opportune for China to Implement Its 'Go Out' Strategy," *Xinhua News,* 11 September 2004 (in Chinese), online at http://news.xinhuanet.com/fortune/2004-09/11/content_1969011.htm, accessed 17 September 2004.

[71] "China Eximbank Held Mid-Year Working Conference of 2004," 16 July 2004, online at http://english.eximbank.gov.cn/info/Article.jsp?a_no=440&col_no=84, accessed 17 September 2004.

mestically and RMB 81 million (US $8.78 million) overseas.[72] TCL took advantage of the situation and started a merger and acquisition negotiation with Thompson. In the end, TCL became a 67 percent shareholder of TTE; Thompson held the remaining 33 percent.

Previously, TCL was a dominant player in China and Thompson was strong in Europe and the United States. In 2004, after the merger, TCL and Thompson together sold 18.5 million color TV sets in 2003, more than any other single company in the world. The merger has combined two regional leaders into a global leader.

In 2002, TCL also purchased bankrupt Schneider, a well-known German name in TV and electronics, mainly for its brand and for access to Schneider's worldwide distribution network. [73]

BOE Technology's acquisition of Hydis. On January 22, 2003, Beijing Orient Electronics Group Co. Ltd. (BOE) acquired Hydis, the flat-panel display business unit of Hynix Semiconductor of Korea, for US $380 million. BOE acquired all of Hydis' thin film transistor–liquid crystal display (TFT-LCD) production lines, all of Hydis' TFT-LCD technologies and patents, and the latter's global sales network.[74]

The new company is called BOE Hydis. According to information provided on its website, it is one of the top ten flat panel display manufacturers in the world (approximately 4 percent of the world's market share).[75] BOE Hydis is headquartered in Korea. The purchase was motivated by the desire to acquire core TFT-LCD display technologies. BOE already started planning to build the fifth-generation TFT-LCD displays based on Hydis technology in Beijing. Note that

---

[72] "World's Largest TV Manufacturer Starts Operation," *People's Daily,* 30 July 2004, online at http://english.people.com.cn/200407/30/print20040730_151340.html, accessed 15 September 2004.

[73] "China's TCL Buys Bankrupt German Schneider," *People's Daily,* 8 October 2002, http://english.people.com.cn/200210/08/print20021008_104620.html, accessed 17 September 2004.

[74] "Clear New Vision for LCD," *China Daily,* 13 February 2003, online at www.china.org.cn/english/scitech/55722.htm, accessed 10 September 2004.

[75] See the FAQ of BOE Hydis, www.boehydis.com/Eng/prcenter/FAQ.asp, accessed 17 September 2004.

the fifth-generation technology is currently the world's most advanced and only Samsung and LG-Philips operate such production facilities.

In addition to mergers and acquisition, Chinese companies have started to establish R&D centers in other countries. Konka, a large Chinese TV manufacturer, has set up an R&D facility in Silicon Valley and Haier has an R&D center in Germany. Huawei, a rapidly growing telecom equipment manufacturer, has invested in several research institutes outside China: Dallas (United States), Bangalore (India), Stockholm (Sweden), and Moscow (Russia).

China's outward FDI is still insignificant compared to the inward FDI to China. However, its impact on China's progress in technology and the global market should not be underestimated.

Global Network of Overseas Chinese

Overseas Chinese played an important role in bringing FDI to China in the early 1980s and 1990s. FDI from Hong Kong, Macao, and Taiwan accounted for more than 63 percent of FDI in 1995 but gradually decreased to around 45 percent in 2000.[76]

Apart from channeling a large portion of FDI into China, both overseas Chinese and returnees have played an important role in introducing high technology and advanced management skills and have often taken prominent R&D or teaching positions in China after receiving education and training abroad.

According to the China Ministry of Education, more than 700,000 Chinese students studied or were studying at overseas educational institutions between 1978 and 2003, and only 172,800 of them have returned.[77] However, with improving economic and research conditions in China, more and more are returning to China.

For example, Shanghai Zhangjiang High Tech Park (SZHTP) has attracted overseas Chinese and returnees to set up two of China's

---

[76] Cheong (2003).

[77] CMOE, *Yearbook of Oversea Students 2003*, 2004, online at www.moe.gov.cn/guoji/cgliuxue/cgliuxue/08.htm, accessed 8 September 2004.

most advanced semiconductor manufacturing plants—SMIC and GSMC—both ranked high in the world in terms of production capacity. The formation and operation of the two companies typify what overseas Chinese can do in bringing advanced technologies, management skills, and international finance back to China. The technological achievements of SMIC and GSMC could not have been predicted five years ago. This shows how China can outperform the expectations of outsiders by taking advantage of the global network.

Saxenian (2003) calls this phenomenon "brain circulation" and concludes that "Overseas Chinese engineers in Silicon Valley created the cross-Pacific collaborations that fuelled Taiwan's emergence in the 1990s as a global center of technology production," and that "regions of China are now poised to repeat Taiwan's experience a decade later, albeit under significantly different conditions."[78]

Overseas talent sourcing is also a key measure to achieve S&T progress in the next ten years, as clearly stated in Foresight 2003 and the 10th Five-Year Plan.

Impact of Foreign Competition

The large influx of FDI into China has resulted in increased competition among foreign companies and also between Chinese enterprises and foreign firms.

Increased competition among FIEs often forces foreign investors to transfer advanced technologies and provide favorable packages to the Chinese partners, as we saw in the GE case above.

On the other hand, Chinese companies have been able to imitate and learn from the foreign competitors in the process of surviving the competition from FIEs. The Chinese TV and home appliance market and PC market are good examples that illustrate this effect. In the late 1980s and early 1990s, Japanese brands—i.e., Hitachi, Sony, Toshiba, and National—dominated the Chinese TV and home ap-

---

[78] Permission obtained from the author to cite this paper.

pliance market to a significant extent. By 1996, the Japanese firms had lost their dominant market position to such Chinese firms as Haier, TCL, Konka, and Changhong.[79]

A Stronger Industrial Sector with an Extensive Global Network

With its extensive global network and strong foreign players, the Chinese industrial sector should not be weak at all in competing with Korean companies. Of course, Korean companies will compete not only with Chinese indigenous companies but also with FIEs and foreign multinational corporations in China.

China has benefited greatly, both economically and technologically, from its increasing openness and the massive inflow of FDI, as well as improved human resources. China's large market has been a major determinant of FDI inflow and has strengthened the Chinese government's bargaining power in the area of technology transfer from foreign investors.

Figure 4.6 attempts to capture the interactions and relationships among Chinese national strategies and goals, NIS, and the foreign sector that we discussed in this chapter.

Evaluation of China's NIS and the Direction of Its Strategy

China's strategic strength lies mainly in its openness as an engine of growth, its strong bargaining power because of its huge domestic market, and its abundance of highly educated workers and researchers. Its vulnerability lies in the fact that its major R&D capability is concentrated in sectors other than industry, which may slow down China's growth in innovation capability. In addition, the Chinese government's strategy of entrusting most of its national R&D

---

[79] "Strategic Implications for Developing Private Enterprises in China," *Industrial and Commercial Daily*, 10 July 2003, online at http://big5.china.com.cn/chinese/OP-c/362981.htm (in Chinese), accessed 20 September 2004.

Figure 4.6
Relationship Among Chinese National Strategies and Goals, NIS, and the Foreign Sector

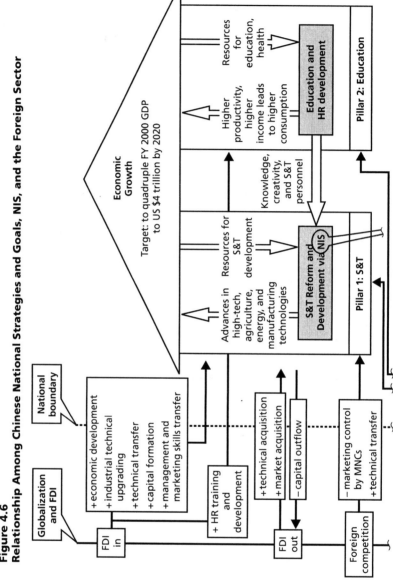

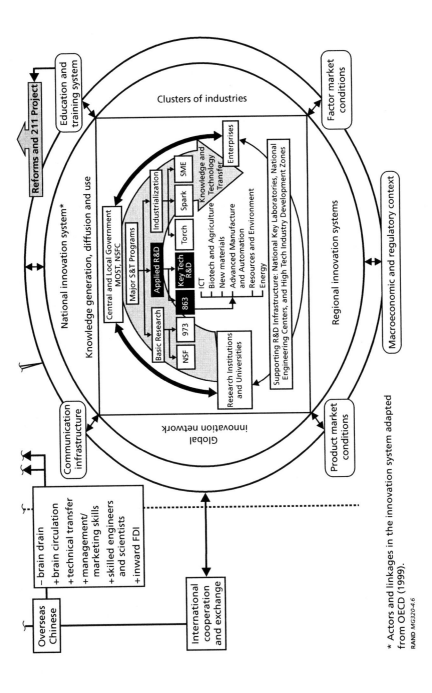

* Actors and linkages in the innovation system adapted from OECD (1999).

RAND MG320-4.6

programs to R&D institutes and universities risks further weakening the link between R&D bodies and market incentives—as well as innovation capability of the enterprises.

It may take a considerable time for China to develop its national innovation system so that China is as efficient as the advanced countries. However, it is on its way to rapid progress in S&T, with a solid conceptual framework, a focused strategy, and a favorable infrastructure and economic environment.

CHAPTER FIVE

Future Prospects and Options for Korea

China has been able to leverage its large and fast-growing domestic market to attract more FDI and MNC R&D centers, bargain for more technology transfer, produce abundant high-quality scientists and engineers, and even pursue its own technology standard. In addition, China's strategy of openness has helped it achieve explosive economic growth and impressive technological progress, even though it is still a socialist country with a less sophisticated market system than some other developing countries.

The limited size of Korea's domestic market, always one of its weaknesses, has driven Korea to pursue an export-oriented development strategy. With the rise of China, however, Korea's outward-looking strategy based on selling commodities to the world does not seem to be enough to secure its future prosperity, because Chinese companies will be in a better position to produce most manufactured goods.

Not only manufacturing but also R&D seem attracted to China's large market and abundant human resources. China is becoming the top destination for overseas R&D by multinational corporations, regardless of its poor protection of IPR.[1]

What can Korea do to ensure its prosperity in the future? In this chapter, we examine where Korea and China have positioned themselves in the technology race, how the future S&T of the two

---

[1] Economist Intelligence Unit (2004).

countries is oriented, and Korea's options for facing the challenges of the future and making the best out of its opportunities.

First, we analyze existing survey results and forecasts concerning the current technology gap. Second, we examine how Korea and China are paving their ways to the future, facing the future that the surveys forecast. Third, we put together the analytical results in the previous chapters, ideas gleaned from the literature, and our understanding of Korea and China to suggest a collection of options from which Korea could choose. The options suggested in this chapter will be grouped into four broader strategies in Chapter Six. In this chapter, we focus on the micro-characteristics of each strategy and the relevance of each strategy as an option for Korea. Our analysis of how the options differ from each other in terms of their effect on Korea's economic performance appears in Chapter Six.

Future Prospects for S&T Progress in Korea and China

In this section, we aim not to forecast the future of Korea and China in terms of S&T capability but rather to draw on existing literature on the technology gap to understand the relative progress of the two countries in S&T. We also analyze how the governments of both countries are preparing for the future because their strategic emphases and resource allocations will influence their future progress in S&T.

Where Is Korea Positioned in the Technology Race?

Existing surveys on the technology gap and technology forecasting are basically dependent on the "best guesses" of expert groups. Because results vary depending on the selection of technologies, the composition of the respondent group, and questionnaire designs, there are substantial limitations to the survey method.

Surveys are difficult and expensive to design and must be carefully conducted to avoid the pitfalls of imprecise definitions and poor communication that fail to convey the essence of the questions. Survey respondents are often poorly informed about the breadth and depth of the subject matter and sometimes lack senior leadership emphasis and resources, which are rarely available.[2] Further, because it is easy for opinion rather than fact to become the basis for survey responses, there is a possibility that the survey will be manipulated by respondents having vested interests in its outcome or that different respondents will use different standards or rules in formulating their responses, thus rendering the results difficult to interpret.

Due to the severe limitations of the existing surveys of technology level assessment, we do not take the survey results of the studies introduced below at face value. We examine and compare different studies for the purpose of getting a better sense of the technology race among countries including Korea and China.

In 2002, 17 ministries of Korea, including KMOST and MOCIE, drew the National Technology Map for Korea's S&T strategy in the next ten years. The National Technology Map derived five visions, 13 development directions, 49 strategic products and functions, and 99 core technologies.

The 2003 Survey of Technology Level by the Korea Institute of Science and Technology Evaluation and Planning (KISTEP) evaluated Korea's relative technology level in the 99 core technologies, compared to those of the world's technology leaders.[3] Korea's technology level on average was 65.1 percent of the U.S. level; Korea was 5.8 years behind the United States. As shown in Table 5.1, of the 13 development directions, Korea is relatively strong in IT-related areas but weak in aerospace. The KISTEP survey shows that Korea is weaker than China in aerospace, as one might have guessed. Interestingly, Table 5.1 shows that the technology gap between Korea and China is widest in the IT-related fields, even though Korea and China are increasingly competitive in IT product manufacturing and trade.

---

[2] This is often because the responses are assigned to more inexperienced members of an organization's staff.

[3] KISTEP (2004b). Article 14-2 of Korea's Basic Law of Science and Technology mandates that KMOST investigate and compare Korea's technology level relative to those of other countries and take measures to improve Korea's technology level.

Table 5.1
Technology Gap Survey Results for the 99 Core Technologies of Korea's National Technology Map

Vision	Development Directions	Korea's Technical Level (%)	China's Technical Level (%)	Gap Between Korea and World's Leaders (years)	Gap Between Korea and China (years)
I	1. Ubiquitous communications	72.9	48.2	3.2	4.1
	2. Contents and service innovation	69.8	50.3	3.5	3.2
	3. Intelligent living environments	73.4	43.8	3.6	4.9
II	4. New medicines (development/ industrialization)	58.7	46.4	5.1	2.0
	5. Prevention of disease, diagnostics, innovations in cures	62.5	49.1	4.8	2.2
III	6. Environmental innovations for a pleasant and healthy life	54.4	48.3	8.8	1.0
	7. Environmentally friendly, efficient, and stable energy supply and demand; energy industrialization	63.3	57.0	6.3	1.0
IV	8. Future transportation equipment and systems	70.5	51.9	7.8	3.1
	9. High-tech dwellings and social infrastructure innovations	69.3	57.4	6.6	2.0
	10. Next-generation production systems/ mechatronics	72.0	51.1	4.8	3.5

Table 5.1—continued

Vision	Development Directions	Korea's Technical Level (%)	China's Technical Level (%)	Gap Between Korea and World's Leaders (years)	Gap Between Korea and China (years)
	11. New materials/ components	72.0	61.1	5.1	1.8
V	12. Entering the era of aerospace	46.5	69.2	11.9	−3.8
	13. Food security/ resource reservation	63.0	50.9	6.4	2.0
	Average	65.1	52.5	5.8	2.1

SOURCE: KISTEP (2004b).
NOTE: The technology level was evaluated by how a country's specific technology of the country compares with the world's technology leaders on a percentage scale. The technology gap measures how many years a country's specific technology is behind the world's best technology holder or the other country in the comparison.

In the sectors the KISTEP survey sampled, the industrial sector was underrepresented. Out of 1,067 experts surveyed, the industrial sector accounted for 17.0 percent, academics for 34.4 percent, and research institutes for 48.6 percent. Considering the fact that Korea is relatively weak in basic science and strong in commercialization, the KISTEP survey results may have a downward bias against Korea.

On the other hand, there is also an upward bias favorable to Korea resulting from the 99 technologies selected. These 99 technologies are either at the infant stage or the growing stage in Korea, while they are mainly growing or mature technologies for the world leaders. In other words, the 99 technologies belong to the next generation of emerging technologies from the Korean perspective but not from the point of view of global technology leaders.

How Does China Evaluate Its Global S&T Progress?
China's National Research Center of Science and Technology (NRCSTD) did a survey similar to KISTEP's as part of Technology

Foresight 2003.[4] The more than 1,000 experts who responded to the survey were asked what the current level of China's R&D was on 222 topics in the three thematic fields of IT, biotechnology, and new materials, in comparison with those of leading nations in technology.

Out of 222 topics, China was five years behind or less on 86 percent, equivalent to the leading nations on 8 percent, and six to ten years behind on only 5 percent. The survey concluded that the technology gap between the world's technology leaders and China on the 222 topics averaged about five years.

This looks more optimistic than the KISTEP survey of China's technology level summarized in Table 5.1, which estimates the technology gap at eight years. This discrepancy might be due to the sampling bias in technology selection.

The 222 topics of the NRCSTD survey were selected either because China has a good chance to develop the technologies in five to ten years or because they are necessary for China's future socio-economic development. Therefore, the choice of the technologies itself explains the technology gap. From the point of view of world technology leaders, China's 222 technologies may have been more geared toward mature technologies than Korea's 99 core technologies in the KISTEP survey.

In addition, most of the NRCSTD survey respondents belonged to academic and R&D institutions; fewer than 5 percent were from the industrial sector. Considering the fact that China's industrial-sector R&D capabilities are quite limited, the composition of the respondent sample also may have resulted in upward bias for China's technology level.

Future Prospects for the Technology Gap Between Korea and China

According to the KISTEP survey, the technology gap between Korea and China is quite narrow, only 2.1 years on average. There are other studies on the technology gap between Korea and China and between Japan and Korea. A recent survey by the Korea Development Bank

---

[4] The technology gap was only one of the questions in the NRCSTD survey; KISTEP (2004b) was confined to the technology-level survey.

(KDB) showed that Korea's technological capability is 3.8 years ahead of China's and 2.2 years behind Japan's.[5] The KDB survey sampled industry experts whose main concern is applied technologies and development. Therefore, the gap between Japan and Korea may have been underestimated whereas the gap between Korea and China may have been overestimated.

How might the relative technological capabilities of Korea and China change in the near future? The KDB survey covered a forecast of the technology gap as well. If Korea's technology level is expressed as 100, then the China's technology level would rise from 76.5 in 2004 to 87.0 in 2007 and 94.5 in 2010; the technology gap between Japan and Korea would also narrow. According to KDB, the technology gaps among Korea, China, and Japan would become much smaller by 2010 but the order would remain the same: Japan first, followed by Korea and China.

However, a survey done by *Nihon Keizai Shimbun* (Japan Economic Newspaper, Inc.) reached different conclusions.[6] It predicted that China's technological capability would be ahead of Korea's in ten years. The respondents of the survey were R&D executives of 439 major Japanese companies. According to the survey, the present technological capability of companies in Japan, Korea, and China was evaluated at 4.0, 3.3, and 2.6, respectively, on a 5-point scale. The survey predicts that ten years later, Japan, Korea, and China will be at 4.1, 3.6, and 3.8 in technological capability, respectively. China will surpass Korea whereas Taiwan will still be behind Korea at 3.1.

Again, the conclusions depend on the selection of industries, among other biases. For example, KDB (2004) predicted that the order of Japan, Korea, and China would be sustained in the industrial machinery industry by 2010. Korea would be still ahead of China in automobiles and computers, while Korea would almost catch up with Japan in those industries by 2010. In consumer electronics, telecom-

---

[5] KDB (2004).

[6] "Formidable Chinese Technology: Technological Capability of China Will Surpass That of Korea in 10 Years," *Chosun Ilbo* (2004).

munications equipment, and the petrochemical industry, the technology gaps among the three countries will be quite narrow in 2010. The KDB survey predicted that Korea will surpass Japan in the semiconductor industry and China will almost catch up with Korea.[7]

How Is Korea Paving Its Way to the Future?

In 2003, the Korean government initiated the Next Generation Growth Engine program to achieve the goal of a per capital income of $20,000 by 2012.[8] Ten "Next Generation Growth Engine industries" were designated based on five selection criteria: (1) global market size of the industry, (2) strategic importance, (3) market and technology trends, (4) Korea's capability to become internationally competitive, and (5) contribution to the national economy.[9] Table 5.2 shows the list of the ten growth engine industries.[10]

Currently the Next Generation Growth Engine Program, together with 6T promotion,[11] is one of Korea's flagship programs in S&T progress within a five-to-ten-year time frame.[12] It accounted for 5.8 percent of the total government R&D budget in 2004. Al-

---

[7] At least in the memory chip market, many experts expect Samsung to maintain its first-rank position for a long time because of entry barriers such as the need for large-scale investment (about $2 billion per product line) and market risks due to demand fluctuations. In addition to Korea and Taiwan, China could have a significant position in the semiconductor market, even with the inherent restriction of export control by advanced countries.

[8] Korea's per capita gross national income was $12,646 in 2003.

[9] In the late stage of the program's establishment, Korea's major traditional industries, such as shipbuilding, iron and steel, textile, and petrochemicals, were excluded from the growth engine industries.

[10] Ministry of Finance and Economy (MOFE) and other 11 ministries, "Enforcement Plan of the Next Generation Growth Engine Program," 22 August 2003, www.most. go.kr/most/t_board_admin_operation.jsp?listID=jungbo13&bSeq=1005970&flag=read, accessed 28 October 2004.

[11] As discussed in the previous chapter, "6T" refers to information technology (IT), biotechnology (BT), nanotechnology (NT), environmental technology (ET), aerospace technology (AT), and cultural technology (CT).

[12] We say "currently" because Korea government has a tendency to change program names or redo medium- or long-term programs before the planning period is over if a new administration comes in.

Table 5.2
Korea's Ten Growth-Engine Industries, 2003

Industry	Products and Technology Examples
1. Digital TV/ broadcasting	Broadcasting systems, DTV, DMB, set-top boxes, complex equipment
2. Displays	LCD, LED, PDP, Organic EL, 3D, electronic paper, related materials
3. Intelligent robots	Domestic service robots, IT-based service robots, robots for extreme work environments, robots for medical supports, generic technologies for artificial intelligence
4. Future automobiles	Intelligent automobiles, environmentally friendly automobiles, intelligent traffic systems
5. Next generation semiconductors	Next-generation memory chips, System on Chip (SoC), nanoelectronic devices, related materials
6. Next-generation mobile telecommunications	4G handsets and systems, telematics, signal handling and interpretation technology, electro-optic telecommunication technologies
7. Intelligent home networks	Home servers/home gateways, home networking, intelligent consumer electronic products, ubiquitous computing
8. Digital contents/ software solutions	Production, utilization, and distribution systems of digital contents, cultural contents, embedded software, intelligent integrated logistics system, GIS/GPS technology.
9. Next-generation batteries	Second-order batteries, fuel batteries, hydrogen energy, related materials
10. Biotechnology: new medicines/organs	New medicine, bio-organs (duplication, transplant), biochips, image diagnostic equipment, medical equipment for elders

most one third of total government R&D goes to the 6T promotion program.

We observed two interesting characteristics in Korea's medium-term S&T strategy as reflected in the Next Generation Growth Engine Program:

- Korea is taking an IT-focused strategy. At least six out of the ten growth-engine industries fall into the IT product category. Two other industries—future automobiles and intelligent robots—are

also highly correlated with IT applications in the industry. Only two industries—next-generation batteries and biotechnology (BT) new medicines and organs—are not in the IT category.
- The emphasis is still on tangible products rather than intangible knowledge goods.

These characteristics reflect (1) the design of the program, which chooses "cash cows" to achieve the goal of $20,000 per capita gross national income (GNI) and (2) the level of Korea's development. In other words, Korean companies are still earning money by selling commodities rather than by providing intangible goods such as knowledge and services as other world technology leaders.

For example, Korea's front-running company, Samsung Electronics, is still a hardware company. Most of Samsung Electronics' revenue comes from such hardware as semiconductors, mobile phones, TFT-LCD displays, consumer electronic devices, and communication devices ranging from phones using Code Division Multiple Access (CDMA), a cellular technology, to mobile phones and networking switches.

In contrast, IBM is no longer a PC company. It sells intangible goods, such as services and software, more than tangible commodities. As of 2003, almost half (48 percent) of IBM's revenue came from global services and 16 percent from software. Hardware equipment, such as PCs, mainframe computers, and semiconductors, brought in only 32 percent of IBM's revenue.

Global coordination or integration of global operations for multinational corporations is a big business for U.S. companies including IBM. In improving efficiency and enhancing productivity, companies in the United States focus on global services, consulting, and software.

Fundamental difference exist between Korea and advanced countries such as the United States in technology concepts and technology usage. Even in the same products, there is a difference in technology content. U.S. customers are basically purchasing the technology rather than the equipment itself. When a U.S. company buys a set of hardware equipment, additional investment in training its staff and coordinating their activities often becomes larger than the cost of the hardware. This is because U.S. companies appreciate and utilize intangible value in service, maintenance, and software. Thus we see that Korean companies and U.S. companies are serving different market segments.

How Is China Preparing for Future Emerging Technologies?

The Technology Foresight 2003 report identified ten topics in which China could achieve major breakthroughs in the next five to ten years. These ten technologies reflect the areas of China's future S&T strength. They were extensively researched either under the 863 Program or under the 973 Program.

It is notable that five out of the ten are in biotechnology, as we see from Table 5.3. As a matter of fact, China is already at the forefront in some areas of biotechnology, such as breeding trans-gene farm crops. In contrast with Korea's strategy of betting heavily on IT, China's ten technologies are more balanced between IT and BT.

Table 5.3
Ten Technologies Where China Is Most Likely to Achieve Major Breakthroughs in the Next Ten Years

Field	Technology
Information and telecommunication	1. Next-generation mobile telecommunication (beyond 3G/ultrawide band)
	2. Next-generation networks
	3. Nanometer chips (targeting 12″ 90/65nm chip technology)
	4. Chinese information processing
Life sciences and biotechnology	5. Functional genomics
	6. Medical biotechnology
	7. Bioinformatics
	8. Functional proteomics
	9. Technology for breeding new trans-gene farm crops
New materials	10. Nanomaterials and nanotechnologies

In terms of relative importance, however, Chinese experts who participated in the Foresight 2003 also ranked information and telecommunication technology as the most important field for China's future development, followed by life sciences and biotechnology and then new materials.

Korea and China Are Similar in Their Preparations for the Future

Both countries believe information technology (IT) is the most important field in terms of payoffs and opportunities. Their choice of technology fields within the IT field is also similar. Three out of the four IT fields that China wants to pursue in the next ten years as shown in Table 5.3 overlap Korea's Next Generation Growth Engine technologies in Table 5.2. This similarity may be natural because global technology and market trends are obviously the same for both nations. What matters, however, is technological content, which could be quite different even for products classified under the same technology category. Currently, Korea may have higher technological content than China in quite a few of technology fields. But it is not certain whether Korea can sustain its technological leadership in those fields.

Options for Korea and Their Policy Implications

Korea does not have the depth of knowledge in basic science or generic technologies that Japan and the United States have. It is relatively good in applied technology and commercialization, but this relative strength in applied technology and commercialization might not be sustainable as a long-term advantage because they are more easily obtained than basic and generic technologies. Especially in China, progress in applied technology and commercialization could be much more rapid than in other developing countries because of such positive drivers as huge FDI, significant training and education by FIEs, and the establishment of R&D centers by MNCs.

In this section we examine the directions Korea could take to make successful progress in S&T. The strategies discussed in this section were inferred logically from the analysis of the previous chapters and from our literature survey.

Fortify Strengths in R&D Intensity but Obtain R&D Efficiency Too

R&D Investment Flow Should Go to Knowledge Stock and to Higher R&D Productivity. High R&D intensity is one of Korea's strengths. However, Korea has a longtime problem of relatively low R&D efficiency.[13] Several factors may have contributed this. As we saw in Chapter Three, the density of scientists and engineers in Korea is not as high as in other industrialized countries, while Korea's R&D intensity is in the highest group. To support intensive R&D activities inside Korea, it would be ideal for Korea to have more high-quality scientists and engineers. However, developing highly qualified scientists and engineers is not a short-term project. Therefore, Korea should not neglect opportunities to build networks with others in the "global brain pool." We will discuss the importance of global sourcing and networking again below.

Another major determinant of R&D efficiency is the level of existing knowledge stock. If the knowledge stock is low, R&D investment flows do not produce as much as in countries with a high knowledge stock. R&D investment is a necessary condition to increase the knowledge stock itself. In other words, to reach a certain level of R&D efficiency, Korea must accumulate knowledge stock, and this in turn will need R&D investment.

Other Determinants of R&D Efficiency: Organizational Innovation and Improved R&D Management Skills. Institutional governance and R&D infrastructure are other determinants of R&D efficiency. Compared with China, Korea has a better market system, stronger linkage between markets and technology, and a more modernized

---

[13] Korea's R&D productivity is lower than the average R&D productivity of OECD countries.

institutional structure. So Korea's R&D efficiency will be higher than China's if other things are equal. If Korea and China invest the same amount of R&D funds in the area where they have similar existing knowledge stock, R&D outcomes or productivity would be probably higher at present in Korea. To maintain this advantage and to further improve the R&D efficiency, Korea needs to make continuous improvements in organizational innovation, R&D management skills, and governance structure.

The Government's Role in Future-Oriented Long-Term Research

Next-Generation Technologies and Generic Technologies

Relatively strong applied technology and commercialization capability are Korea's current strengths. However, Korean companies are weak in generic technologies, which are a rich source of intellectual property. Since generic and future-oriented technologies usually involve externalities that cannot be appropriated by invested parties, industries often underinvest in those technologies. This is all the more so in Korea because only a few Korean firms are capable of investing in generic technologies. Smaller firms not only cannot launch such projects but also cannot utilize the results fully even if they succeed in the project. Generic technologies and technologies that will be realized in the long term are areas where the Korean government might want to play a more dominant role.

Due to the program's very design, the Next Generation Growth Engine industries and related technologies derived at the national level are geared toward IT and short- or medium-term technological targets. For the short term, going with products and technologies that will come to fruition sooner may be a lucrative strategy.

However, for the medium and long term, the Korean government might want to pay more attention to technology areas where government needs to play a leading role, such as generic technologies and long-term future technologies in which the Korean industrial sector is less interested. For example, in the 6T promotion program, the

Korean government may want to monitor the project portfolios closely in terms of realization time, risk, and different dimensions of impacts of the technology.

Supporting basic science is another area where government traditionally plays a leading role. In fact, investment in basic science has been rapidly growing in Korea during the last decade. It will take a long time for Korea to join the world leaders in basic science so that it can serve as a foundation for creating next-generation technologies and intellectual property rights. The Korean government may want to put a high priority on consistently moving ahead in basic science and generic technology.

Although China emphasizes the link between technology and markets, China's government R&D is clearly focused on such future-oriented technologies as biotechnologies, new materials, and communication technologies, as we saw from Technology Foresight 2003.

From an IT-Focused Strategy to Diversification into Biotechnology and Nanotechnology

Korea has a relatively sound capability in selected areas of information technology, although it is still quite weak in other emerging technologies, such as BT and nanotechnology (NT). For example, NT is expected to revolutionize science and consumer products over the next two decades the way computers and the Internet have over the past three decades.

In the short to medium term, Korea's current IT-focused strategy may pay off better. For the long term, however, Korea may be better off to gradually diversify into such non-IT areas as BT and NT, which are the core technologies of the next wave of the technology revolution after the IT revolution of the 1990s. Given the scope of this report, we could not do a quantitative analysis of whether an IT-focused strategy is a better option for Korea than moderate diversification into non-IT areas. However, this is an interesting subject for future research.

Accelerate the Pace of S&T Progress Through More Active Global Networking

Try to Become Integrated into Core Groups of Experts in Emerging Technologies. Using Korea's relative advantage in selected areas of IT as leverage, the Korean government, academics, and industry may want to try to become partners with global leaders in S&T and industry. For example, many experts, including a local expert at RAND, believe that a combination of IT, BT, and NT would be a lucrative long-term area of focus for Korea. At present, however, Korea does not have the critical mass of knowledge necessary to pursue such a goal. How could Korea be integrated into the network of core experts in emerging critical technologies, even though it is a weak knowledge creator in those fields?

One option is to invest in networking with core expert groups in the world by sharing projects, encouraging coauthorship with Korean experts, and by securing joint ownership of the intellectual property rights that would result from projects funded by the Korean government.

International collaboration on research and development is a well-known way to take advantage of international knowledge flows. Another effect of tapping into global brainpower would be to introduce greater competition in the market for highly educated human resources in Korea.

"Go Global" with Government R&D Programs. Korean companies are already going global in research. The government could engage in similar activities in R&D to draw on the world's brain pool and existing knowledge stocks. This could be especially effective in fields where Korea has little accumulated knowledge.

To a certain degree, foreign experts should be encouraged to apply for participation in major Korean government R&D programs. The Korean government may want to seriously consider providing extra incentives for foreign participants and coauthorship and co-ownership of the resulting IPR.

The Korea Ministry of Science and Technology is now in a position to lead and guide investments in global networking both in industrial R&D and government R&D. Making government R&D

programs more open to world-class scientists and engineers could help Korea catch up in areas where it is weak and prepare for the next wave of the technological revolution.

Should Korea Be More Engaged in the China Market?

Engaging with China and Taking Advantage of China's Strength

Korea has the option to complement its weaknesses by tapping into China's strengths. Abundant human resources for both production and R&D and a large and a fast-growing domestic market are China's most salient strengths—strengths Korea does not have. Such strategies as inducing foreign investors in China to source from Korea or finding complementary markets with China have been widely discussed in the existing literature in Korea.

Korea has been going in this direction already by investing in China, producing in China, and conducting R&D in China. Proximity to China is another factor that has strengthened the economic relationship between Korea and China. As long as their economic environments are in harmony and the mutually beneficial economic relationship between the two countries is sustained, this would be a good bet for Korea. However, we are not sure what the net effect of greater engagement with China will be in the future.

How Much Should Korea Focus on the China Market?

Will Korea continue to enjoy economic opportunities in China? Could there be a "boomerang effect" from China? Could China carve out a portion of the world market and exclude Korea? These questions represent part of Korea's conflicting perceptions about China. This statement by Ulrich Schumacher, the CEO of Infineon, describes these mixed feelings:

> China is a big question mark. Is it the market of the future? Is it the enemy of the future? Will these people kill you if you help them develop an industry? No one has a clear understanding of

what is going to happen, but one thing is clear: you can't ignore them. Somehow you have to be part of the game.[14]

There is no straightforward answer to the question of whether Korea would be better off by engaging with China as much as it does now, more than now, or less than now. In the next chapter, we show how the answer changes as economic variables and parameters change.

According to our conversation with several R&D managers of research laboratories in China operated by several of the world's leading technology companies, engaging in China is definitely a superior option. In other words, they believe the payoffs of an engagement strategy will be much greater than any negative repercussions from China—whatever they might be—unless an extreme economic situation were to develop in the future. We will explore this conjecture as part of our scenario analysis in Chapter Six.

Diversifying into Other Geographic Markets, Especially Advanced Countries with More Sophisticated Demand

Many in Korea believe that Korean companies should move up the value chain and increase the technological content of their products as fast as possible. If this hypothesis is correct, Korea would probably be better off to explore more challenging markets with more sophisticated customers than those in China. In the scenario analysis, we will explore to what extent this may be so.

Since the mid-1990s, Korea has been exporting more to developing countries than to advanced countries. So far, focusing on markets in developing countries has not been a bad strategy due to the extremely fast-growing China market and the relatively decent performance of other developing countries. However, will these trends be sustained in the long run? The answer will again depend on what kind of future Korea will have. In certain situations, Korea's

---

[14] M. Clendenin, "Let China's Fabs Have Top Technology, Says Infineon's Schumacher," *EE Times*, 27 February 2003, online at www.eetimes.com/article/showArticle.jhtml?articleId=18307999&sub_taxonomyID=2511, accessed 8 August 2004.

focus on markets in China and other developing countries may necessitate some trade-offs between current profits and future opportunities.

Education for Creativity and Innovative Thinking

Reform the Formal Education System to Promote Creative Learning

Because Korea has now achieved a certain level of development, it needs creative and innovative thinking more than the capability to absorb existing knowledge. Educational reform at all levels—primary, secondary, and tertiary—is required for creative learning. This is an important issue in Korea, but it has not yet been well addressed.

The educational effort of most Koreans, especially at the secondary level, is oriented toward college entrance exams and admission—even though official goals are not. This inevitably breeds uniformity and inflexible mindsets. Reforming the curriculum and the orientation of its educational system has long been at the top of the policy agenda in Korea. However, Korea's educational reform is not progressing as rapidly as many stakeholders wish. It has become mired in disputes among different interest groups—preparatory schools for examinees, regular public and private schools, teachers' associations, parents, and different government ministries.

Develop Highly Qualified Scientists and Engineers by Supporting Broader Access to Higher Education

Under the current administration of President Roh Moo-hyun, Korea aims to be an economic regional hub in Northeast Asia. In the area of S&T, Korea wishes to be an "international center of S&T and engineering excellence." An adequate supply of highly educated and trained researchers is one of the necessary conditions to make this dream come true. However, both the number and density of scientists and engineers in Korea are lower than those in Japan and other advanced countries such as the United States.[15]

Korea's ratio of scientists and engineers to the total number of higher education degree holders was 41 percent in 2003, which is significantly higher than that of the United States, Japan, and many other industrialized countries. However, its density—the number of scientists and engineers per 10,000 population—is lower than that of other advanced countries. This is mainly because the ratio of highly educated people to the total population is lower in Korea. Therefore, continued support for broader access to higher education should increase the density of scientists and engineers in Korea.

In addition, the quality of graduate-level education needs more attention.[16] Compared to that of advanced countries, graduate-level education in Korea is quite underdeveloped, even though it has been improving recently. The Korean Ministry of Education and Human Resource Development has put a great deal of effort into its "BK 21" project to improve graduate education in the 21st century.

Education to Overcome the Dichotomy of Growth and Distribution

Developing a well-educated, versatile workforce that is able to conduct R&D and convert it to innovation could serve as a win-win solution to the current confrontational relationship between business and labor. Labor unions in Korea are known as highly confrontational, and Korea's average wage rate is more than ten times that of China.

The trade-off between growth and income distribution has long been a controversial issue in Korea. The Next Generation Growth Engine Program, which sets the goal of a per capita income of

---

[15] Since Korea is a less populous country than either Japan or the United States, we use the density measure to control for the population size difference.

[16] Korea's graduate-level education is regarded as internationally less competitive than its undergraduate level education. This is confirmed by a majority of education experts both inside Korea and abroad.

$20,000 by 2012, and implementation of the new five-day work week[17] are two recent events that have intensified the controversy.

Korea's educational strategy could connect the knowledge-intensive industrial activities of the demand side with the more expensive (relative to China) but highly skilled labor force from the supply side. Ideally, Korea might want to aim for a society in which its citizens are paid as much as those with similar education and skills in advanced countries instead of targeting a specific level of per capita income. To achieve this goal, however, both business and labor need to be more innovative so that Korea's labor productivity will be as high as that in advanced countries.[18]

Other generic strategies to improve quality of S&T education include raising the quality of mathematics and science education in primary and secondary education, emphasizing natural science and engineering training, encouraging lifetime education, and encouraging on-the-job training.

Investment Beyond Production and Technology

Understanding the Uses of Technology and the Subtleties of Customers' Needs

Gurus of the international business community often point out that Korean companies are usually good at mass production of standardized products such as memory chips and liquid crystal displays (LCDs) but are weak in making innovative products, mainly due to a lack of ability to understand the nuances of the market. As Korean companies move up the value chain ladder and move toward more differentiated product markets, they will need, in addition to creativity and technological ability, the ability to understand how to use

---

[17] Until the five-day work week was introduced in 2004, the official work week was five and one-half days.

[18] Labor unions in Korea usually assert that innovative businesses should pay higher wages to their employees. To justify higher wages, however, the labor force needs to be just as innovative and productive. Education could play an important role for both sides.

these technologies. Without that capability, it will be difficult for Korean companies to enter a new market ahead of other competitors.

Lack of understanding the uses of technology and weakness in capturing the subtleties of customers' needs are linked to the product portfolios of major Korean companies. Many Korean IT companies produce standardized products, such as semiconductors and LCDs, that do not necessarily require such nuanced understanding of customer preference. Automobiles are another major Korean export, but Korean automobile companies are not yet strong in sophisticated high-end automobiles and components. Among many factors, Korean companies' relative lack of market sense keeps them from providing innovative products ahead of their competitors.

To complement these weaknesses, Korean companies might want to invest in understanding the use of technologies and the needs of their customers. Another option could be becoming active in strategic alliances and joint ventures with other market leaders in the world to reach target markets by establishing overseas research laboratories, design centers, and marketing research centers.[19]

At the country level, the Korea Ministry of Science and Technology, as a coordinator of microeconomic policy under the new policy governance, could lead investment beyond manufacturing-oriented R&D activities through its S&T programs.[20]

Selling Knowledge Versus Selling Commodities

In many advanced countries, the manufacturing industry is not a major source of income any more. In the United States, manufacturing was responsible for only 14 percent of GDP and 15 percent of employment in 2001.[21] Advanced countries with higher income levels

---

[19] For example, Honda leads the automobile market even in the United States. Honda makes innovative products because the company understands the market and the needs of its customers. Japanese companies usually have design centers and other marketing research groups in the United States.

[20] Refer to Chapter Four for major factors in the new governance of S&T policy in Korea.

[21] Bureau of Economic Analysis (2002).

depend on selling knowledge and investing in the best opportunities rather than selling commodities.[22]

In contrast, Korean governments, as well as those of other developing countries, still tend to focus on selling commodities and to keep their capital inside the country rather than finding the best opportunities worldwide. For example, to address Korea's recent speculation in Korea's overheated real estate market in the era of low interest rates, the Korean government announced traditional measures such as tax disincentives rather than broadening investment opportunities for Korean households through such means as new financial products linked to international assets or allowing them to find the best international investment opportunities.

Given Korea's target per capita income of $20,000 within the next ten years, not only industry but also government may need to move more toward a global business paradigm. Korea may be better off seeking the best international opportunities not only to sell commodities but also to invest wisely.

Better Living Environments to Compete for, Maintain, and Recruit International Experts

The textbook assumption of labor immobility does not hold any more. Highly educated personnel, in particular, are more mobile than others, and competition among countries to retain scientists and engineers and other high-quality human resources continues to increase. Under the Initiative of Northeast Asian Economic Hub, Korea is trying hard to recruit R&D centers and high-value-added activities of multinational corporations. To achieve this goal, the Korean government may need to pay greater attention to making the country an attractive place to live.

---

[22] According to OECD (1999b), the annual growth rate in the services trade between 1990 and 1998 was 6.4 percent whereas that of the merchandise trade was 5.9 percent. In OECD countries, FDI in services was higher than FDI in manufacturing from the 1990s on. Major FDI in services was in banking, business services, telecommunications, and retailing. Companies such as IBM and GE generate about half of their revenues from services.

Openness May Have to Be Korea's Strategy No Less Than China's

Few countries remain economically isolated now that China has opened its doors and other former socialist countries have also made the transition to a market economy. However, in the eyes of foreign investors, Korea is still a hostile country for foreign investment. Many foreign business leaders think Korea is relatively isolated from active global networking.

For example, India takes over $100 billion in business from global software outsourcing by 185 Fortune 500 companies, according to the UNDP (2001). Both India and China have strong links with Silicon Valley, and the further development of information technology will continue to enhance the ability of multinational corporations to tie together globally distributed laboratories and firms. However, even with its world penetration of broadband Internet services, Korea has not yet carved out a significant market in the Internet or software business.

Korea is a small country with a limited domestic market and is less attractive to foreign investors than China, Hong Kong, or Singapore. Therefore, Korea must emphasize both looking outward to explore opportunities on the world market and looking inward to bring in investment and business activities from abroad.[23]

Openness, both inward and outward, may need to be Korea's strategy even more than China's. The Korean government may want to adopt policy initiatives described succinctly as follows:

- Reach out to gain the world's best investment opportunities.
- Reach out to the world-class pool of human resources.
- Let capital and labor go abroad to find the best possible investment and job opportunities.
- Become more integrated with the world.

---

[23] Currently, the Regional Economic Hub Initiative emphasizes bringing in FDI and recruiting R&D centers and experts more than outward-directed activities.

Summary of the Options and Their Linkage to the Next Chapter

The options discussed above can be grouped into four major categories:

- Keeping the current strategy of extensive economic engagement with China and focusing on IT related technologies
- Seeking openness in various directions including more flexible movement of capital and human resources inward and outward. This strategy might include diversifying away from China
- Emphasizing activities to build up R&D and commercialization capabilities and to accumulate knowledge stock
- Focusing on education to develop more abundant and innovative human resources.

In the next chapter, we will analyze the above four strategies quantitatively and look at how each strategy could make a difference in terms of Korea's per capita income in the next ten years, taking into account the deep uncertainties of the future.

CHAPTER SIX
Future Scenarios

This chapter considers how future developments may affect outcomes for Korean economic growth in light of the factors discussed in the preceding chapters. Rather than present a handful of narrative scenarios, we will attempt to lay the foundation for a quantitative analysis that will use scenarios to illuminate issues and prospects for Korean policy choice.

Using Scenarios Analytically

The previous chapters discussed with great specificity elements of the national innovation systems of China (People's Republic of China, or PRC) and Korea (the Republic of Korea, or ROK) and the outputs from each country's innovation enterprise. The discussion also considered the effects of these activities on economic outcomes at the sectoral level and on the economic relationship between the two countries. In the course of this discussion, it has been natural to raise hypotheses and conjectures about the future course and trends of these conjoined systems. Naturally, normative questions about desirable policy alternatives either in light of or seeking to direct future outcomes also arise.

Although this chapter cannot provide the same level of specificity as preceding chapters, it can serve as an initial exploration of variables that decisionmakers in Korea must consider when contemplating the longer-term future. Therefore, this chapter seeks to fulfill three purposes.

The first is to introduce the concept of searching for and selecting among alternative strategies not on the basis of optimality tuned to an assumed "most likely" future or small set of alternative scenarios, but rather as a way to find strategies that appear to be robust—that is, to fulfill certain minimal criteria for success—across a wide range of uncertainties. It is customary to deal with uncertainty by making simplifying assumptions. This chapter, however, seeks to do the opposite and construct an analysis by explicitly making the underlying uncertainties the focus of attention. In this sense, the chapter serves as a basic introduction to the style of analysis that is necessary for considering the effect of near-term actions on long-term outcomes when prediction is not credible.[1] These concepts will be treated in greater detail in the third section of this chapter.

Our second purpose is to lay the groundwork for more definitive research to follow. Beyond the didactic purpose of providing a general introduction to robust decision methods, this effort represents the first steps in applying robust decision analysis to the profound questions of strategy facing Korean decisionmakers in an era of potentially great change and deep uncertainty. It is our hope that this analysis can be modified and expanded in later work.

Finally, we seek to provide what might best be termed a stylized analysis of the choices facing Korean policymakers. Because of the preliminary and exploratory nature of this work, undue weight cannot be placed on the results at this time. Nevertheless, we hope to present an initial sense of what changes might make a difference to Korean prosperity and provide an ability to explore the relative magnitude of their possible effects.

---

[1] For a more detailed discussion of the themes and analytic issues touched on in this chapter, see Lempert, Popper, and Bankes (2003).

A Simple Model of Korea's National Economy

A robust decision analysis of choices facing economic decisionmakers in Korea requires a means for generating scenarios in a systematic and purposeful fashion. We offer in this chapter a simple model to serve as such a tool. It is intended to provide a backbone that can support later development and more detailed structure.

In its basic form, it begins with the simple accounting identity for ROK national income:

$$Y = C + I + G + X - M \ . \qquad (6.1)$$

We wish to explore the interplay between two bodies of phenomena and the policy choices that surround them. The first is the effect on the Korean economy of a primary focus on the rapidly growing export market in the PRC. The second is to understand how this choice of focus may be supported—or its possible downside consequences offset—by changes in national innovation system investment in the ROK and the degree to which the outputs of this investment may be utilized. To do so, we will extend the basic equation, Equation 6.1, in several directions.

The Role of China in Korea's Future

To capture the central role played by Korean exports to China, we modify Equation (6.1) above is as follows:

$$Y = C + I + G + X_{ROW} + X_{PRC} - M \ . \qquad (6.2)$$

That is, we disaggregate exports into those directed toward the PRC and those that go to the rest of the world.

On the supply side, the Korean GDP production function is taken to be:

$$Y - X_{PRC} = A K^a L^{1-a} RD^b .$$
(6.3)

This is the standard Cobb-Douglas production function that has been modified to account explicitly, on the input side, for the effect of investments in research and development for the output of the Korean economy, and on the output side to delete the exports to China. We modify the work of Shin (2004) to derive the following empirical relationship:

$$\ln (Y - X_{PRC}) = -7.6735 + 0.3524 \ln(K) + 0.6476 \ln(L) + 0.1389 \ln(RD) .$$
(6.4)

This relationship makes use of the elasticities derived from the above-cited work. The value of A has been chosen to yield the observed result for 2003, the last full year for which data are available, for the value $Y - X_{PRC}$. In other words, running Equation (6.4) on the appropriate values for 2003 will yield the actual result for Korean GDP for that year minus the value of goods exported to the PRC.

From the work of Yang (2004) we took the following relationship:

$$X_{PRC} = f (GDP_{PRC}, FDI_{ROK\ PRC}, WPY, DUMMY_{1998}) .$$
(6.5)

This work found that the key variables that explained the observed time series for Korean exports to the PRC (XPRC) are Chinese GDP, the amount of foreign direct investment by Korea in China (FDIROKPRC), the exchange rate between the Korean won and the Japanese yen (WPY), and a dummy variable that takes on the value of 1 for the extraordinary year, 1998, but is elsewhere held at zero. Estimating this relationship for the data available to us yielded the following results:

$$\ln(X_{PRC}) = -5.6149 + 0.8745 \times \ln(GDP_{PRC}) +$$
$$0.4221 \times \ln(FDI_{ROK\ PRC}) +$$
$$1.1202 \times \ln(WPY) - 0.3924 \times \qquad . \qquad (6.6)$$
$$DUMMY_{1998}$$

The R^2 for this regression is 0.98. All coefficients behave as expected and are significant to at least the 90 percent level. Using the values generated by Equation (6.6) and adding the results to those derived from Equation (6.4) therefore provide a model for estimating the effects on future Korean GDP of changes in the external environment and of future outcomes stemming from present policy choices.

The Need for Sustaining Technological Levels

We now introduce one further change for the sake of illustration. Since we are interested in the issue of relative technical development, we would like to have the single demand-driven element in the simple Korean economic model be dependent to some degree on the relative technology levels of the PRC and the ROK. Our proxy for this stock factor is the ratio of annual expenditures on R&D as a fraction of total GDP. In 2002, as noted above in Table 3.2, these ratios were 1.23 and 2.91 respectively for the PRC and the ROK. The data presented in Table 3.3 suggest that this ratio has been increasing at an astonishing rate in the PRC, on the order of 14 percent per year. It is most likely that the relative ratio between the ROK and the PRC will experience a decline from its 2002 value of 2.37 (i.e., 2.37 = 2.91/1.23). The argument of the preceding chapters is that this narrowing would most likely have a negative effect on Korean exports to the PRC.

To represent this effect, we return to Equation (6.6). One of the determinants of Chinese demand for Korean exports is the term WPY, the current-year average won/yen exchange rate. That is, as Korean goods become cheaper relative to those of a principal competitor (Japan) in the supply of higher-value-added products to the Chinese market, they should appear relatively more attractive, all things being equal. But what if things are not equal? If the relative technological levels of the PRC and the ROK narrow, as measured by the simple proxy of the R&D/GDP ratio ("R&D Intensity"), then Korean goods would be less likely to find a ready market in a China better able to supply its own needs for such products through domestic production or more attractive foreign imports.

We represent this effect by modifying a single term in Equation (6.6). We substitute the current WPY term for a new one incorporating the concept of an effective won/yen exchange rate as a representation of the relative attractiveness of Korean products:

$$\ln(\text{WPY}_{\text{effective}}) = (1 - \Phi((\rho_{2002} - \rho_{\text{current}}) / \rho_{2002})) \ln(\text{WPY}). \quad (6.7)$$

The symbol ρ represents the ratio between Korean and Chinese R&D intensities as measured by the share of GDP devoted to R&D. Once again, we emphasize that this is nothing more than a stylized representation that provides an expedient means to explore the effect of various external variables on future Korean GDP.

The effect stemming from the dynamics of change in technological level is just conjecture. It does make intuitive sense and certainly captures an important argument used in policy considerations among Korean policymakers. Yet the extent to which it might actually affect the export of Korean products in the future is presently unknown. Rather than merely assume that the trade effects of declining technological level do—or do not—occur, in the spirit of a robust decision analysis we explicitly represent this uncertainty over the magnitude of the effect as opposed to making assumptions ex ante for the sake of computational tractability. For this purpose, the term Φ appears in Equation (6.7). It takes on a value from 0 to 1. If the value is 0, it represents the condition where the effect of changes in relative R&D intensities, ρ_t, is minimal or nonexistent. When the value of Φ is 1, it represents a state of the world where the posited effect actually appears with full force. Having introduced this concept, we can then explore what effect this structural uncertainty may have on the choice of strategic direction, in addition to the parametric uncertainties already discussed.

The Nature of the Korean Labor Force

Two further extensions to the basic model have been introduced to capture several of the concepts considered in the preceding chapter. A detailed discussion of these concepts may be found in Appendix A. For the purpose of following the analysis, however, we discuss them briefly here.

The labor force in Korea has been posited to grow at the same rate as population. However, we have included the possibility that, as the result of strategic policy decisions, the labor force grows at a rate that either outpaces or lags the growth of the population as a whole. Therefore, the model includes a "Job Creation Rate" that takes on the value of zero if the labor force grows at the same rate as the general population. It may also take on other values as an additive increment to that basic population growth rate. This value is subject to control through policy choices made by decisionmakers.

Similarly, we have also introduced the concept of an "Adjusted Labor Effect." This was done to simulate the potential for qualitative or institutional changes in Korea that would lead to a measurable increase in the productivity of the labor force. These would include changes in the legal and institutional structure regarding entrepreneurship, for example, as well as changes in the nature or level of education and training of workers. If the value of this variable is set at 1, there is no change in the productive power provided by the Korean labor force. Any higher value would act as a multiplier on the effective size of the labor force and hence on productivity contributed by the actual labor force.

Strategies and Scenarios

Analytical Models and Policy over the Long Term

Equations 6.1–6.7 provide a simple, abstract representation of the Korean economy.[2] Although we began with concepts of demand in Equation (6.1), the heart of the model is the simple supply-driven production function of Equation (6.4). From this we have disaggregated only one demand element, namely Chinese demand for Korean goods and services. The simple model is largely free of feedback loops that are characteristic of any economy. Most notably, Korea's trade with the rest of the world is subject to an implicit assumption of ceteris paribus—i.e., all other things remain equal. No demand shocks from that quarter can be represented directly.

Clearly, the limitations of the model make it inadequate for prediction. The central argument of this section, however, is that even if the model were considerably more complicated to almost any conceivable degree, it still could not generate reliable predictions for a decade from now. Try as we might, we are not capable of creating simulations of a complex and adaptive system, such as an economy placed within a larger environment of other world economies, that will yield reliable predictive outputs. Large and well-refined macro-models cannot be entirely accurate in predicting even one year into the future—to say nothing of a decade or more. Viewed in this light, there is no a priori evidence that the simple model presented above would necessarily perform worse than models of considerably greater sophistication. That being the case, it is worth asking what use our model or, indeed, any model of the Korean economy can be for illuminating policy choices.

Economic models are created to play a role in the "predict-then-act" process of economic analysis. Traditional model use has been governed by a strategy of analysis that instructs us to develop the most apposite and accurate possible model of the system of interest, to use that model to generate predicted outcomes, and then to apply

---

[2] These represent the core equations. The additional equations required to have a fully functional model system are presented in Appendix A.

the tools of optimization to find the best single course for action. Is this a reasonable use of an economic model, however, when prediction is not credible? If we have optimized for one, supposedly most-likely, future and the actual future turns out differently, we can hope that our previously optimal plan will still be serviceable—but we have no actual proof or theorem that this will, indeed, be the case. We might find ourselves bound on a course that is clearly deleterious to our interests given the way the state of the world has changed from what had been expected.

This observation raises the question of whether we even ought to be interested in prediction in the first place. That is, predictions themselves are not our end goal. Rather, we wish to understand how changes in the future might affect our choice among alternative short-term actions today and how the actions we do take will affect our chances of being successful in meeting our goals in the years to come. In other words, our true interest is not so much in predicting the future. Rather, realizing that we cannot be sufficiently predictive, we seek some means to understand how we can choose today's actions most wisely in light of our long-term objectives.

The logic of the analysis we present below is that it is not sufficient to optimize strategy for one assumed set of conditions in the presence of the deep uncertainty that surrounds long-term planning and analysis. Rather, the goal should be to seek those strategies that might not be optimal in any given future but are likely to prove robust. That is, they will achieve certain minimal criteria set by the planners, across a wide range of plausible states of the world. In this case, what we need from a model is not a prediction. Rather, a model serves as an artifact that contains what we understand about critical relationships among key factors and that can then be used to generate the myriad scenarios of the future that are consistent with our current information. As we systematically vary the values of factors whose future values are presently unknowable, we generate an ensemble of alternative futures purposefully constructed so as to act as a test bed for helping select among policy alternatives. Rather than characterizing uncertainties at the beginning of the analysis either by assigning values, assuming probability distributions, or dropping them entirely pending later analysis, we leave the uncertainties uncharacterized in terms of probabilities but nevertheless explicitly represent them in the model. In effect, we are now asking which uncertainties would affect our decisions today and how certain values of these presently uncertain factors might affect our choice among actions.

Four "Strategies" for Korea

In this analysis in particular, we posit four strategic choices for Korean national planners. These are summarized in Table 6.1. It is important for the reader to bear in mind that although the strategies have names like "R&D"[3] or "Education," all should be considered

Table 6.1.
Alternative Strategies for the Korean Economy

Effect	Strategy			
	Base	Openness: Refocus Attention Away from China	Focus on R&D	Focus on Education
Knowledge base growth rate	10%	10%	**13%**	10%
Capital investment rate	27%	**29.7%**	27%	27%
Commit to exporting to China	1.0	**0.6**	**0.8**	**0.8**
Job creation rate	0.01%	0.01%	0.01%	**0.02%**
Speed of narrowing the technology gap between Korea and China	−0.05%	−0.05%	**−0.03%**	−0.05%
Adjusted labor effect	1.0	**1.02**	1.0	**1.03**

NOTE: Input values that differ from those of the base case are shown in boldface.

---

[3] We retain the quotation marks in the names of each strategy to remind the reader that although these names are evocative of actions being discussed in Korean policy circles today, they are by no means to be taken as definitive representations either of these policy alternatives or the potential outcomes.

mixed strategies of varying policy elements. The names merely characterize the strategies by referring to the central element in each. For example, the "R&D" strategy must necessarily also include education elements but to a lesser degree than the "Education" strategy.

The four alternative strategies are characterized by the effects they would have on crucial model inputs if they were to be put into practice.[4] We will first characterize these input effects. The detailed descriptions for each are to be found in Table 6.2.

The first strategy listed in Table 6.1 is termed "Base." The values for each of the input effects listed along the rows are those that are presumed to hold, on average, over the entire time course of the analysis if no decisions were taken to move Korean economic development off the path it is presently following. For each of the subsequent strategies, these values would change. The changes from

Table 6.2
Description of Model Input Effects

Effects	Description
Knowledge growth rate	Average annual rate of growth of the base of R&D inputs to production
Capital investment rate	Average annual rate of investment in capital
Commit to PRC exports	Share of the potential for exports to PRC as calculated in Equation 6.6 actually realized each year
Job creation rate	Rate at which jobs are added to the economy in excess of the rate of population growth
Change in R&D intensity rate	Rate of change in the ratio between Korean and PRC R&D intensity
Adjusted labor effect	Effective increase in the productive capacity of labor due to changes in education, training, institutional changes, etc.

[4] Given the simplicity of our present model, we could not model the effect of certain policy decisions endogenously within the model. Rather, what we have done is to stipulate that certain policy decisions have been taken that result in the intermediate outcomes shown in Table 6.1. For the present, we assume that any chosen policy is successful in meeting the goals chosen for it as shown in the table. In a fuller robust decision analysis, this assumption could also be represented explicitly to examine the implications for meeting long-term goals.

the "Base" strategy are indicated by boldface entries in the relevant cells of Table 6.1.

The "Openness" strategy presumes two fundamental changes. The first is that decisions are taken to change Korean institutions and policies to make the economy more open to foreign investment, both direct and indirect, and to encourage Korean producers to look to other, more challenging, external markets. The second change is a consequence of the first, namely a shifting of attention away from China as the crucial market focus. The net results of these changes in strategy are reflected in the cells in the "Openness" strategy column in Table 6.1. As a result of more FDI, average annual investment in capital would increase. Further, the adjusted effect on labor would be positive because of increased opportunities for learning occasioned by more foreign access, improved intellectual property protection, increased opportunity for observing foreign best practice, etc. However, the price of this increased openness and refocusing is that less emphasis, fewer resources, and reduced policy attention is given to achieving the maximum potential exploitation of the PRC market. The lack of a component for modeling demand in the rest of the world limits the potential gains from this strategy as well as additional sources of shock to the Korean economy.

The "R&D" strategy also has two principal beneficial effects and one deleterious one. Here, the decision is made to invest more of national income in building the R&D stock. As a result, the rate of change of relative R&D intensity between the ROK and the PRC becomes less unfavorable to Korea's relative technological superiority. The result should be a better competitive posture in the Chinese market (and the rest of the world) as well as enhanced domestic productive capacity. But, as above, the refocusing comes at a cost. Again, the level of potential exports to the PRC has been scaled back to reflect that under this strategy resources and high-level attention are directed into other sectors. Still, the penalty is less than in the case of the "Openness" strategy.

The final strategy posits that resources and policy attention are given to increasing human capital in Korea through a greater investment in education and training. This is presumed to yield a greater stimulus in creating job openings in the Korean economy because a concomitant change in institutions makes individuals more capable of exercising entrepreneurship and accelerating the growth of small start-up ventures. Similarly, the adjusted labor effect is enhanced by having Korean workers who are better educated, more skilled, and more creative than was formally the case. As above, this emphasis comes at a price modeled by a change away from a singular focus on developing the Chinese market for Korean goods and services.

Analytical Results

Strategy Performance Under Different Assumptions

We begin our analysis at the place where most other analyses of the traditional sort would conclude. Figure 6.1 compares the four strategies by calculating what the average annual rate of growth in GDP per capita would be for South Korea during the period leading to 2015 if each strategy were pursued under the same conditions—namely those that we have termed the nominal case.[5] The values for input parameters constituting the nominal case are shown in Table 6.3. Unlike the inputs governed by the four candidate strategies, these values are assumed to be influenced by factors exogenous to our model and by policy decisions other than those reflected in the strategies we focus upon.

The values of output in 2015 from each strategy under the nominal case conditions are shown as black bars in Figure 6.1. Under these conditions, the average annual rate of growth in GDP per capita of the current "Base" strategy, about 2.75 percent, would dominate those for the other three strategies. Similarly, if all values were held constant but we assumed that China's growth rate accelerated considerably to an average of 12 percent per year over this period (as

---

[5] This figure and the ones to follow are snapshot captures of computer screens from the exploratory modeling program used to carry out the analysis.

Figure 6.1
Comparing 2015 Values of GDP per Capita Following Four Strategies

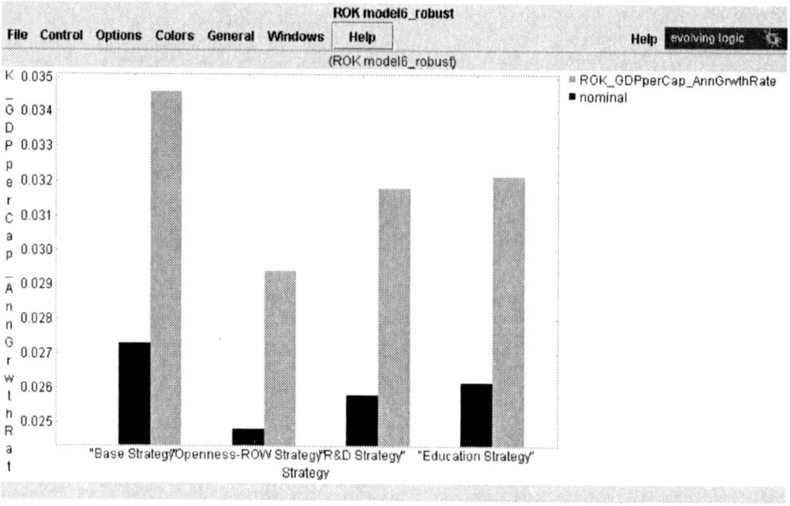

represented by the gray bars) and that Korean FDI in China matched this level, the "Base" strategy would clearly be the course to follow, at least according to this single metric for judging future outcomes.[6]

In Figure 6.2, we take a similar view. Again, for purposes of comparison, the nominal set of assumptions yields the results shown in black for each strategy. Now, however, we seek to simulate the result for each strategy in the case of serious prolonged stagnation in Chinese growth. This value is now set at 3 percent per year, with Korean FDI in China similarly scaled back. Under these circumstances, represented by the light gray bars in Figure 6.2, the "Base" strategy's outcome would be overtaken by the performance of both the "Education" and "Openness" strategies in the same circumstances.

---

[6] This rate of average annual growth is almost beyond serious consideration—almost. We pick this value to illustrate how wide the boundaries can be placed when creating ensembles of plausible future states of the world in the search for robust strategies.

Table 6.3
Nominal Case Values for External Uncertainties

External Uncertainty Factor	Description	Nominal Case
PRC_GDP_Growth_Rate	Average annual rate of growth in PRC economy	9%
PRC_KFDI_Growth_Rate	Average annual rate of growth in Korean FDI investment in PRC	9%
Won/Yen_Appreciation_Rate	Average annual rate of won/yen appreciation	–2%
Capital_Depreciation_Rate	Average annual depreciation rate of Korean capital stock	7%
ROK_Population_Growth_Rate	Average annual rate of population growth in Korea	0.62%
Days_Work_per_Year_ROK	Average number of days worked per member of Korean labor force	260
Technology_Differential_Effect	Value of Φ, measuring degree of importance of technology differentials in trade with PRC	0

Figure 6.2
Comparing 2015 Values of GDP per Capita Under Different Assumptions

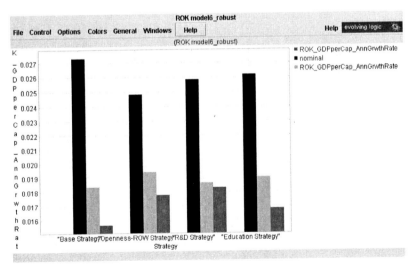

We can go further. If we assume that both Chinese growth and Korean FDI remain unchanged throughout the period until 2015 at 9 percent—the nominal case represented by the black bars, we can then examine the effect of changing the nominal case assumption about the importance of the narrowing technological differential between Korea and China. To do so we change the value of the term Φ appearing in Equation (6.7) from 0 to 1. This now represents the condition where the plausible effect of changes in relative R&D intensities indeed has full force and is shown in the figure by the dark gray bars. In this case, we see that even though Chinese growth and Korean FDI remain quite robust throughout the period at 9 percent each, the "Base" strategy now finishes in last place. Growth in Korean GDP per capita would be less than if any of the other strategies were followed. In the situation of stagnant Chinese growth (light gray bars), the "Openness" strategy would be preferred. When the technology effect is fully felt, even if Chinese growth remained robust (dark gray bars) the "R&D" strategy would be preferred.

Exploring the Implications of Uncertainty

Views of the sort shown in the preceding figures provide the crucial insight that changes in assumptions may lead to major swings in recommendations about which policies to pursue. Clearly, we need to understand more. In Figure 6.3 we examine in detail the behavior of one strategy, the "Base" strategy. Inasmuch as this strategy most closely represents current Korean policies, it is important to examine where its vulnerabilities might lie.

Figure 6.3 reports the performance of the "Base" strategy in each of 100 different scenarios. Our previous examination showed that among the unknowns, variations in the value of Chinese GDP growth and in the value of the factor Φ, which measures how fully the technology differential effect takes hold, have a substantial effect on outcomes. Our 100 scenarios, therefore, are defined by holding all other terms constant but varying along the horizontal axis different future rates of Chinese economic growth and along the vertical axis different possible values, from 0 to 1, of the technology differential effect term from Equation (6.7). The simulated outcome from ap-

Figure 6.3
Outcome of "Base" Strategy Across 100 Scenarios

ROK model6: ROK_GDPperCap_AnnGrwthRate

File Control Options Colors General Windows Help   Help evolving logic

(ROK model6: ROK_GDPperCap_AnnGrwthRate) nominal

	-0.01	0.00	0.01	0.02	0.03	0.04	0.05	0.06	0.07	0.08	0.09	0.10	0.11	0.12	0.13
1.0	0.013	0.013	0.014	0.014	0.014	0.015	0.015	0.016	0.016	0.017					
0.9	0.013	0.014	0.014	0.014	0.015	0.015	0.016	0.016	0.017	0.018					
0.8	0.014	0.014	0.014	0.015	0.015	0.016	0.017	0.017	0.018	0.019					
0.7	0.014	0.015	0.015	0.015	0.016	0.017	0.017	0.018	0.019	0.02					
0.6	0.015	0.015	0.016	0.016	0.017	0.018	0.018	0.019	0.02	0.021					
0.5	0.015	0.016	0.016	0.017	0.018	0.019	0.02	0.021	0.022	0.023					
0.4	0.016	0.016	0.017	0.018	0.019	0.02	0.021	0.022	0.023	0.025					
0.3	0.016	0.017	0.018	0.019	0.02	0.021	0.022	0.024	0.025	0.027					
0.1	0.017	0.018	0.019	0.02	0.021	0.023	0.024	0.026	0.027	0.029					
0.0	0.018	0.019	0.02	0.021	0.023	0.024	0.026	0.028	0.03	0.032					

Y-axis: ech_Differential_Effect (1.1 to -0.1)
X-axis: PRC_GDP_Growth_Rate

Legend:
>= 0.028
>= 0.025
>= 0.02
>= 0.015
< 0.015

RAND *MG320-6.3*

plying the "Base" strategy in each of these scenarios is reported in each cell. These values are then shading-coded according to a scale in which white represents rates of average annual growth equal to or above 2.8 percent across the entire period through 2015 whereas black, on the other end of the scale, represents those falling below 1.5 percent.

What Figure 6.3 shows is not too surprising given what we have seen so far. The "Base" strategy performs best when Chinese growth is the highest and the technology factor carries the least weight. It seriously underperforms when Chinese growth stagnates and the technology factor has the most weight.

The values on the two axes were deliberately chosen to span the full range of plausible possibilities. This strategy serves two purposes. The first is that one can logically argue that any conclusions we can draw based on this ensemble of future scenarios is quite likely to be true of whatever future actually transpires because we have deliberately chosen to describe an ensemble that is almost certain to include the true future values within it. The second purpose is a bit more subtle. By making the values on the axes so inclusive, we ensure that the views and assumptions of the widest range of interest and researcher communities have been incorporated. That is, we avoid the usual ex ante arguments about assumptions that attend most analytic exercises. Each group can usually find a point on a landscape such as the one shown in Figure 6.3 where its views are represented and given equal weight with all others. In fact, particular cells could be labeled as representing a particular scenario consistent with that assumed by such-and-such a ministry or such-and-such an analyst. In this way, the analysis can proceed with all parties agreeing on its core validity.

The analytical value of such a "landscape" view is that it can be used as a tool that allows us to reason from an ensemble of scenarios in a disciplined manner rather than considering only a few chosen unsystematically or based upon administrative or other pressures. In particular, we can ask what the effect on these results would be if we varied other variables being held constant. We can also compare similar landscapes for the other strategies. For example, Figure 6.4 shows the same output as in Figure 6.3, but this time assuming that the "R&D" strategy is played out across the level playing field of 100 selected scenarios. In this view, we can see that this strategy also performs rather well in the region where the "Base" strategy is strong. In addition, the "R&D" strategy appears to fail less grievously in those regions of the landscape that are a serious obstacle for the "Base" strategy. Nowhere in this region does the "R&D" strategy produce an average annual rate of growth in GDP per capita of less than 1.5 percent. The "Base" strategy, by contrast, produced 19 such outcomes in the 100 scenarios we examined.[7] By contrast, each strategy produced a similar number of instances where this rate was in excess of 2.5 percent per year on average. The reason the "Base" strategy dominated "R&D" in the bar chart of Figure 6.1 was because in that particular scenario, represented by the (0.9, 0.0) ordered pair and indicated by

---

[7] Note that rounding up for the sake of the figures produces cells where the actual result is less than 1.5 percent but the value ".015" is shown in the cell.

Figure 6.4
Outcome of "R&D" Strategy Across 100 Scenarios

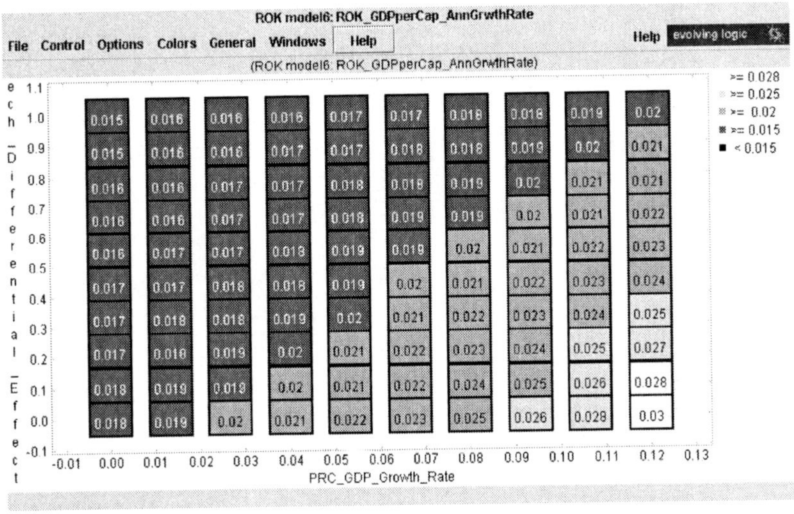
ROK model6: ROK_GDPperCap_AnnGrwthRate
File Control Options Colors General Windows Help
Help evolving logic
(ROK model6: ROK_GDPperCap_AnnGrwthRate)
>= 0.028
>= 0.025
>= 0.02
>= 0.015
< 0.015
ech_Differential_Effect
PRC_GDP_Growth_Rate

RAND *MG320-6.4*

the dark box around the corresponding cells in Figures 6.3 and 6.4, the average annual rate of growth for the former was 2.8 percent while the latter was 2.6 percent.

Toward Robust Strategies in the Face of Deep Uncertainty

With Figures 6.3 and 6.4, we begin to see what it would mean to use robustness as a criterion for selecting strategies, as opposed to optimization for particular assumed conditions. A robust strategy might not produce the same level of achievement in a particular state of the world as another strategy that would be optimal for those precise circumstances, but it may provide greater assurance of meeting some minimally acceptable result across a wider range of plausible future states of the world. In this sense, to seek robustness is to search for hedges against an uncertain future by shaping a wise policy course. To use a robust decision analytical approach is to construct such a hedge in a systematic and quantitative fashion.

It is possible to address the issue of robustness more directly. In Figure 6.5 we run the same simulations as those in Figures 6.3 and 6.4. However, in this case the value in each cell now reports the relative regret of pursuing the strategy being modeled. The *regret* of pursuing a strategy is measured by the difference between the result of a chosen strategy in a specified state of the world and the result that would be obtained if the optimal strategy for those circumstances had been pursued. Therefore, if the strategy being examined would, indeed, be the optimal strategy for a particular state of the world, the regret would be 0. If that strategy is not optimal for those circumstances, there would be measurable regret. Relative regret divides the regret result by the value of the outcome yielded by the optimal strategy. *Relative regret*, therefore, gives the percentage reduction of the value of the optimal result that is the cost of having pursued the chosen strategy instead.

Figure 6.5
Regret of the "Base" Strategy in 100 Scenarios

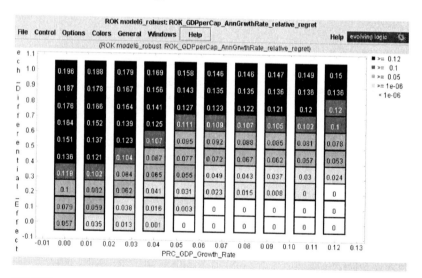

In Figure 6.5, those scenarios where the "Base" strategy is optimal have cells colored white. The relative regret is 0. Those scenarios where the "Base" strategy would not be optimal but the resulting forgone annual growth in GDP per capita would be within 5 percent of the result for the optimal strategy in each such scenario have cells shaded the lightest gray. Those cells where the relative regret is within 10 percent of the optimal are medium gray. Those less than 12 percent are shaded in dark gray with white numerals. And for scenarios where the "Base" strategy results in regret of 12 percent or more in forgone growth in GDP per capita when compared to the optimal strategy for that case, the cells are colored black.

This regret landscape for the "Base" strategy indicates what we would expect but now gives us a much better sense of context. Rather than illustrating a single point outcome, we have a landscape within which to view that outcome in relation to all others. In this case, the greater the rate of growth of the PRC economy, the better this strategy performs. However, the greater the demand placed on technological value-added—that is, as the value of the technology differential effect approaches 1—the greater the challenges for this strategy. The potential gain is large. In nearly 30 percent of the futures portrayed, this strategy performs best or within 5 percent of the strategy that would have been optimal for that future. But the potential costs of being trapped in a world where China's growth is stagnating while greater technology performance is being demanded are also quite large.

Similar relative regret maps for the other strategies are shown in Figures 6.6, 6.7, and 6.8.

The "Openness" strategy essentially bets against continued PRC economic growth in preference to more focus on the rest of the world and so prospers best when Chinese growth is weak, as shown in Figure 6.6. It does progressively less well as this bet against the PRC fails to match the actual performance in more optimistic scenarios for that country.

By the same token, the regret landscape for "R&D," shown in Figure 6.7, suggests that this strategy works well in a situation that

Figure 6.6
Regret of the "Openness" Strategy in 100 Scenarios

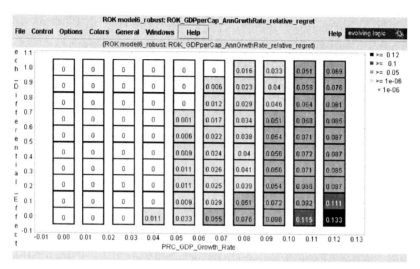

Figure 6.7
Regret of the "R&D" Strategy in 100 Scenarios

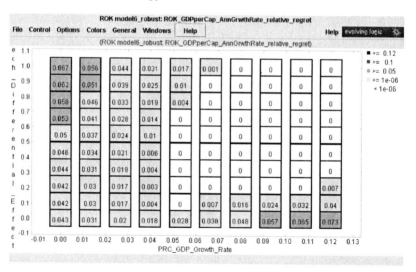

Figure 6.8
Regret of the "Education" Strategy in 100 Scenarios

ROK model6_robust: ROK_GDPperCap_AnnGrwthRate_relative_regret

File   Control   Options   Colors   General   Windows | Help | Help [evolving logic]

(ROK model6_robust: ROK_GDPperCap_AnnGrwthRate_relative_regret)

■ >= 0.12
■ >= 0.1
✳ >= 0.05
  >= 1e-06
◆ < 1e-06

e c h	D i f f e r e n	t i a l E f f e c t									
1.1	0.089	0.085	0.081	0.076	0.071	0.065	0.073	0.083	0.093	0.103
1.0	0.085	0.08	0.075	0.07	0.064	0.063	0.072	0.081	0.09	0.1
0.9	0.08	0.075	0.069	0.063	0.056	0.06	0.069	0.077	0.086	0.095
0.8	0.074	0.068	0.062	0.055	0.049	0.056	0.064	0.072	0.079	0.087
0.7	0.067	0.061	0.054	0.046	0.043	0.05	0.057	0.064	0.071	0.077
0.6	0.06	0.053	0.045	0.036	0.036	0.042	0.048	0.054	0.059	0.065
0.5	0.052	0.044	0.035	0.026	0.027	0.031	0.036	0.041	0.046	0.05
0.4	0.043	0.034	0.024	0.014	0.015	0.018	0.022	0.026	0.029	0.039
0.3	0.033	0.023	0.013	0.002	0	0.009	0.02	0.031	0.041	0.051
0.2	0.022	0.011	0	0	0.011	0.023	0.033	0.044	0.053	0.062

-0.01   0.00   0.01   0.02   0.03   0.04   0.05   0.06   0.07   0.08   0.09   0.10   0.11   0.12   0.13

PRC_GDP_Growth_Rate

RAND *MG320-6.8*

causes stress to the "Basic" strategy—namely, when both PRC economic growth (representing a large potential for gain) and the demands of technological differentiation (representing a large hurdle to overcome in exploiting this potential gain) are high. The strategy also behaves nicely in most of the other regions and really only suffers greater loss when either the PRC market dries up (in the upper-left corner) or the lower right where the PRC market is booming, but the opportunity cost of having invested in R&D in such an undemanding environment takes a toll.

Finally, the regret map for the "Education" strategy, Figure 6.8, shows only one scenario where it would be optimal. It does show serious regret in the upper-right-hand region, but exhibits mild regret elsewhere.

Challenges to Robustness and Characterizing Uncertainties

Based upon the analysis so far, the "R&D" strategy emerges as a candidate for being the basis of a robust policy. Among the scenarios displayed in Figure 6.7, it is the optimal strategy for the broad central region and exhibits only mild regret, being within 5 percent of the achievements of the optimal strategies in those scenarios where the "R&D" strategy is not yet optimal. In fact, out of our 100 spanning scenarios, the "R&D" strategy is either optimal or comes within 5 percent of the optimal values in 91 scenarios.

This analysis is by no means conclusive, however. At this point those employing a robust decision methodology would proceed in several directions. These steps would include the following:

- Performing similar examination of each strategy's behavior by varying different assumptions than those that have been shown in the preceding four "landscape" regret map views
- Conducting systematic computer searches for stressing futures for the candidate robust strategy and then comparing its performance with that of the other potential candidates
- Developing more fully and with greater sophistication aspects of the scenario generator (that is, the underlying model) that the preliminary analysis on the simple model will have shown to be of special importance to understanding and selecting among possible actions
- Modifying the candidate robust strategy to strengthen it in those regions that computer search has shown would lead to unacceptable results, perhaps through hybridization with aspects of the other candidate strategies or introducing a priori rules for adaptation based upon signposts discovered through the computer search
- Throughout the process, integrating the insights of analysts and experts on the relative importance of plausible scenarios.[8]

---

[8] One of the strengths of the robust decision approach is that it permits the incorporation of knowledge that is not usually incorporated easily into other quantitative methods. In this case, for example, while one strategy may show a serious weakness in some scenarios it still might be preferred to one that did middling well in all scenarios because the people associated with the analysis would have knowledge that the troubling scenarios are really not credible based on qualitative knowledge that they possess.

The essence of the analytic strategy at this point is to continue to reduce the vulnerabilities of the candidate strategy as far as possible. That is, through increasingly sophisticated policy design and refinement of the scenario-generating model against which it is tested iteratively, winnow down the list of uncertainties to which the candidate robust strategy would be vulnerable. Finally, the irreducible uncertainties can be presented to the final decisionmakers along with a characterization not so much in terms of their likelihood but rather in terms of their effect on the final decision for action. The analysis does not exist as a separate step before the point of decision: The decision to be informed is the central feature of the analysis throughout.

Challenge Scenarios to Probe Robustness of Candidate Strategies

The analysis reported in this chapter did not proceed to the later stages listed above. Yet, it is possible to engage in some initial explorations. For example, what would be the robustness properties of the "R&D" strategy that performed so well, given the nominal case values for external factors, if conditions were less favorable?

Figure 6.9 portrays the same situation as shown in Figure 6.7 but with the following differences. Instead of continued long-term engagement in the PRC, annual Korean FDI growth shrinks from 9 percent to 1.3 percent. The won appreciates rapidly against the yen at a rate of 3.2 percent per year. The rate of capital depreciation within Korea itself accelerates to 9.2 percent per year from the 7 percent level. And the Korean population increases more rapidly moving from 0.62 to 0.84 percent growth per year.

These values were chosen principally to find a possible future that was most stressful for the "R&D" strategy. We are attempting to find possible failure modes for the candidate strategy. However, while these conditions would represent a clear break from present trends, they could be consistent with the potential influence of an external shock, such as a collapse or near-collapse of the regime in North Korea. This would presumably be attended by in-flows of population to South Korea, marked shifts in investment away from China to

Figure 6.9
Regret of "R&D" Strategy in Stressful Futures

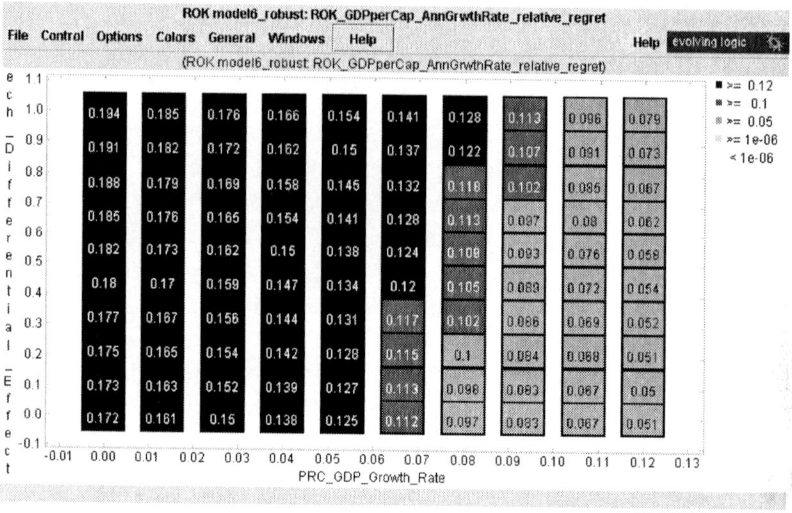

north of the DMZ, and an acceleration of depreciation of capital as the process of adjustment takes place. Therefore, while a surprising set of circumstances, these values are plausible given our present information.

As we can see from Figure 6.9 when compared to the nominal case scenarios of Figure 6.7, the changes we have outlined would have a profound impact on the relative regret of having pursued the "R&D" strategy across 100 scenarios.[9] This illustrates once more that actual conditions in the future may invalidate the assumptions upon which a particular policy course may have been chosen. Hence, there is value in considering the robustness properties of any course of action.

---

[9] It should be understood that we are now showing in these views 100 new scenarios that differ from the 100 we showed before because we have varied the assumptions in the manner described in the paragraph.

What would have been the better strategy to follow under these conditions? Figure 6.10 shows the analogous relative regret landscape for the "Openness" strategy. Clearly, given the almost uniquely disastrous external circumstances shown by setting the conditions above, turning Korea's back on China and pursuing the "Openness" strategy, as defined in this analysis, would be optimal in all scenarios. Bear in mind that this figure only shows the values of relative regret. "Openness" would do better than any other strategy under these circumstances; this is not to say that these outcomes would be good by an objective standard.

We can also proceed in the opposite direction. What if at the same time the "R&D" strategy was being pursued, Korea also engaged in a more proactive manner with the PRC? Here, the nominal case as been changed by increasing the growth of Korean FDI in China to 12.7 percent from 9.0 percent per year. We also posit

Figure 6.10
Regret of "Openness" Strategy in the Same Futures As Shown in Figure 6.9

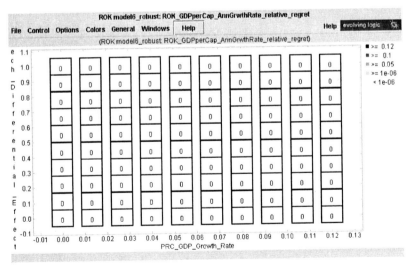

accelerated appreciation of the yen versus the won due to Japanese recovery. The resulting relative regret has been shown in Figure 6.11. Note, however, that this tends to enhance the robustness properties of this strategy when compared to the base case shown in Figure 6.7 because in our simple model we do not track the opportunity cost of the investment resources that might otherwise have been spent domestically or used in more progressive engagement in more challenging markets than that of the PRC.

We can now see what would be the relative regret of the "Openness" strategy under these changed circumstances. This is shown in Figure 6.12. Clearly, the "Openness" strategy, as we have characterized it for the purposes of this study, is by no means a universal panacea. Still, it clearly remains the optimal strategy in those circumstances where the PRC does exhibit catastrophic stagnation.

In the examples above, the analyst manually constructed best and worst case scenarios. A robust decision methodology requires more systematic approaches, and the computer provides the means

Figure 6.11
Regret of "R&D" Strategy Under Favorable Circumstances

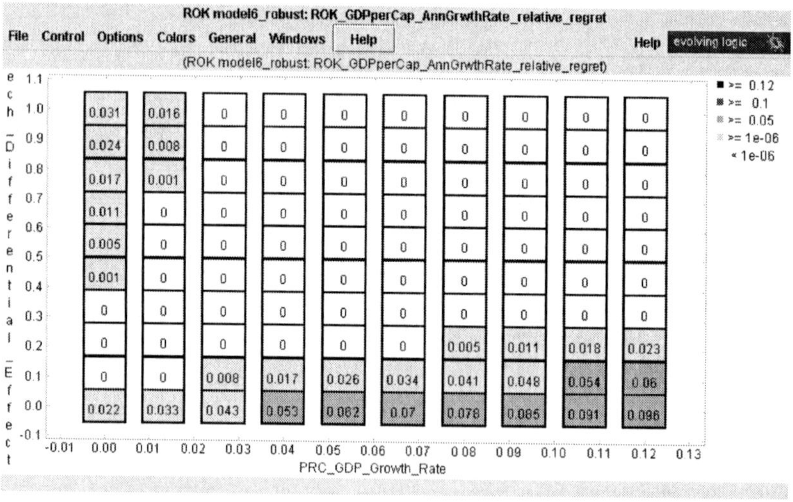

RAND MG320-6.11

Figure 6.12
Regret of "Openness" Strategy in the Same Futures As Shown in Figure 6.11

ROK model6_robust: ROK_GDPperCap_AnnGrwthRate_relative_regret

File   Control   Options   Colors   General   Windows   Help   Help   evolving logic

(ROK model6_robust ROK_GDPperCap_AnnGrwthRate_relative_regret)

Legend: ■ >= 0.12 ■ >= 0.1 ■ >= 0.05 >= 1e-06 < 1e-06

Tech_Differential_Effect (y-axis) vs PRC_GDP_Growth_Rate (x-axis)

y										
1.1	0	0	0	0.018	0.036	0.055	0.075	0.095	0.115	0.135
1.0	0	0	0.009	0.026	0.045	0.064	0.093	0.103	0.122	0.142
0.8	0	0	0.016	0.034	0.052	0.071	0.09	0.109	0.128	0.146
0.7	0	0.006	0.023	0.04	0.059	0.077	0.095	0.113	0.131	0.148
0.6	0	0.011	0.028	0.045	0.063	0.081	0.098	0.115	0.132	0.148
0.5	0	0.015	0.032	0.048	0.065	0.082	0.099	0.115	0.13	0.145
0.3	0.002	0.017	0.033	0.049	0.065	0.081	0.096	0.111	0.125	0.138
0.2	0.003	0.018	0.033	0.048	0.063	0.077	0.096	0.115	0.133	0.149
0.1	0.001	0.016	0.038	0.06	0.082	0.102	0.121	0.138	0.154	0.169
0.0	0.02	0.043	0.066	0.088	0.108	0.127	0.144	0.16	0.174	0.186

x-axis: -0.01 0.00 0.01 0.02 0.03 0.04 0.05 0.06 0.07 0.08 0.09 0.10 0.11 0.12 0.13
PRC_GDP_Growth_Rate

RAND MG320-6.12

for doing so. In particular, we have constructed computer searches to find especially stressing futures for each strategy. The computer did searches over an experimental design[10] running 1,000 selected cases for each strategy for a total of 4,000 simulation scenario runs.

Table 6.4 describes the results from this simple, relatively small sample experiment. For each strategy, the variables describing the input variables for the worst case found are shown. For the "Base" case, the combination of slower growth rate in the PRC, high weight on technology differential effects, appreciation of the won against the yen, and a relatively high rate of population growth in Korea serve to depress the value of GDP per capita in the end year. The "Openness"

---

[10] The experimental design selected was the so-called Latin Hypercube. In this experimental design, both the number of desired simulations and the number of variables to search over are set by the operator. Other variables are held fixed. The computer will then select variable values to uniformly sweep the hyper-volume described by conceptualizing the selected variables as the dimensional axes spanning this space and the end point values of these variables as the length of each axis.

Table 6.4
Worst Cases Found for Each Candidate Strategy Among 1,000 Simulations

	Strategy			
	Base	Openness	R&D	Education
Input Values				
PRC_GDP_Growth_Rate	0.006	0.112	0.021	0.007
PRC_KFDI_Growth_Rate	0.02	0.113	0.036	0.02
Won/Yen_Appreciation_Rate	0.027	-0.036	0.026	-0.023
Ave_Ann_Depreciation_Rate	0.08	0.093	0.098	0.099
ROK_Population_Growth_Rate	0.01	0.002	0.007	0.004
Tech_Differential_Effect	0.98	0.066	0.383	0.935
Outputs				
ROK_GDP_EndYear	819.999	854.227	716.36	708.26
ROK_GDPperCap_EndYear	1.52E+04	1.73E+04	1.37E+04	1.40E+04
ROK_GDPperCap_AnnGrwthRate	0.016	0.026	0.007	0.009
ROK_PRC_Exports_EndYear	8.797	143.858	17.249	10.787
Rel_R&D_Intensity_EndYear	1.214	1.214	1.592	1.214
ROK_Population_EndYear	54116709	49506451	52422872	50575283
ROK_L_EndYear	24992780	23044994	24280599	23548385
ROK_GDPperCap_AnnGrwthRate_relative_regret	0.189	0.18	0.277	0.088
Best_Strategy	Openness	Base	Openness	Openness

strategy is defeated in ideal conditions for the "Base" strategy, and so forth. It is interesting to note from this small sample that in three of the four worst cases, the best strategy would have been "Openness."

These results are merely representative. Even for a relatively simple model such as the one used as the scenario generator in this analysis, a very large number of scenarios would need to be examined to learn the systemic failure modes for each strategy. Fortunately, this task can be completely computerized. Ideally, in the course of one hour, over 700,000 scenarios could be simulated with the scenario generator used in this chapter. The actual exercise will be left for later analyses.

Discussion and Conclusions

The analysis presented in this chapter is by no means conclusive. We have deliberately chosen not to carry the robust decision analysis to a conclusion because of the risk of placing undue weight on a particular solution given the simple nature of the model being used. Rather, the analysis constitutes a first step toward taking the themes, issues, and data presented in the earlier chapters and tying them dynamically into a systematic procedure for the analysis of appropriate policies for Korea. Extensions of this model, such as introducing more demand elements specifically for exports to the rest of the world and introducing budgetary constraints beyond the notional form in which they currently exist, would permit the analysis to probe more deeply and derive more definitive conclusions.

Beyond the general purpose in carrying the discussion to this point, the analysis does suggest in broad outline several of the strategic courses that might be open to Korean decisionmakers. At least in this simple and admittedly abstract analysis, Korea's current course, characterized as the "Base" strategy, seems to have great potential for sustained growth under favorable conditions. However, it also seems to be fragile to several potential shocks—in the form of developments in the PRC that might lead to drops in GDP growth—as well as to the more gradual but foreseeable processes that might cause the technology differential between the two countries to narrow.

In contrast, the "R&D" strategy seems to show promise as the basis for a candidate robust strategy. Maintaining a technical advantage over China—or at least keeping the technological gap between Korea and China as wide as possible—could be an insurance policy against stressful times in the future and could maintain the relative attractiveness of Korean products if there were a downturn in China's economic development. And though not specifically modeled in this exercise, it would also give Korea a greater opportunity to explore and develop a presence in more challenging markets.

Of course, this study has necessarily simplified our four strategies. The strategies are characterized as presumed results from various policies, and these results, in turn, serve as inputs to the model. A more detailed analysis would seek to expand the model serving as the scenario generator by developing endogenous relationships that would represent processes by which the actual instruments of policy, such as greater government investment and various fiscal measures, would yield those outcomes—subject, as always, to both exogenous and endogenous uncertainty. Uncertainty, too, would need to be incorporated into later models. Exploring the strategies in this manner would highlight the value of their most important elements and serve as a means to make concrete some of the qualitative issues that are being discussed in Korea.

CHAPTER SEVEN

Conclusion

This study has attempted to identify Korea's main economic concerns related to China's rapid industrial development and growing science and technology (S&T) capabilities and to show alternative S&T strategies that Korea may follow and how those strategies can make a difference to Korea's economic prosperity.

Korea's economic concerns regarding a rising China lie in the uncertainty of whether Korea could maintain its market position in both the Chinese and world markets as China becomes more competitive in industries where Korea currently has a relative advantage. Korea has a niche in the Chinese market in terms of price competitiveness. However, this niche might become less secure as competition in the Chinese component and equipment market increases. In addition, combining advanced technologies of their own and cheap and disciplined labor in China, world-class companies may create new markets and remove Korea from the market niche it now enjoys.

Our evaluation of China's current S&T capability could be summarized as "limited R&D capability with increasing potential." S&T input and output indicators show that China has made significant progress in terms of growth on all indices. However, it also faces significant challenges because of scarce investment resources and relatively low invention and innovation capabilities.

China's strategic strength lies mainly in its openness as an engine of growth, its strong bargaining power resulting from a huge domestic market, and its abundance of highly educated human resources. On the other hand, the vulnerability of China's national innovation system lies in the fact that its major R&D capability is concentrated in sectors other than industry. Universities, research institutions, and government laboratories are the main R&D performers and innovators in China, even though they may not respond to market incentives as effectively as industry. This may leave China in the situation of being less active in market-driven IPR activities for some time to come.

Recognizing the weakness in "demand pull" factors due to relatively weak industrial R&D capability, the Chinese government has tended to entrust most of the national R&D programs to R&D institutes and universities. This strategy may risk further weakening the link between R&D bodies and market incentives as well as the innovation capability of the enterprises. It may take a considerable time for China to develop its national innovation system to become as efficient as those of advanced countries.

China is not only the manufacturing powerhouse of the world but is also becoming the top destination for overseas R&D by multinational corporations, despite its poor protection of IPR. Not only manufacturing but also R&D activities are attracted to China's large market and abundant human resources. China is making rapid progress in S&T, with a solid conceptual framework, a focused strategy, and a favorable infrastructure and economic environment.

What can Korea do to ensure its prosperity in the future? Korea does not have the depth of knowledge in basic science or generic technologies that Japan and the United States have. It is relatively capable in applied technology and commercialization, but this relative strength might not be sustainable as a long-term advantage because applied technologies and commercialization capability are more easily obtained than basic and generic technologies. In China, especially, progress in applied technology and commercialization could be much more rapid than in other developing countries because of such positive drivers as its huge FDI, significant training and education by FIEs, and the establishment of R&D centers by multinational corporations.

Korea's strengths lie in its high R&D intensity, relatively strong industrial R&D capability with quite a few companies that are global innovators, its relatively well-developed market system, and its modernized institutional structure. Korea's vulnerabilities stem mainly from its weakness in basic science and generic technologies, its lack of educational creativity and reform, its limited number of highly qualified scientists and engineers, its limited domestic market, and its weak global networking.

Strategies for Korea

This study has suggested four basic strategies for Korea:

Support R&D Intensity but Obtain R&D Efficiency Too

High R&D intensity is one of Korea's strengths. However, Korea has a problem with relatively low R&D efficiency for a long time. Several factors may contribute to this. As we have seen in Chapter Three, although Korea belongs to the highest group of countries in terms of R&D to GDP ratio, the density of scientists and engineers in Korea is not as high.

To support its intensive R&D activities, Korea will need more high-quality scientists and engineers. This, of course, cannot be achieved in the medium term. To correct this weakness, Korea must build networks with others in the "global brain pool."

Another major determinant of R&D efficiency is the level of existing knowledge stock. If the knowledge stock is low, R&D investment flows do not produce as much as in countries with a high knowledge stock. R&D investment is a necessary condition to increase the knowledge stock itself. In other words, to reach a certain level of R&D efficiency, Korea must accumulate knowledge stock, and this in turn will need R&D investment.

Engage with China

Korea has the option to complement its weaknesses by tapping into China's strengths. Abundant human resources for both production and R&D and a large and a fast-growing domestic market are China's most salient strengths—strengths that Korea does not have. Such strategies as inducing foreign investors in China to source from Korea or finding complementary markets with China have been widely discussed in the existing literature in Korea.

In fact, Korea has been heading in this direction already by investing in China, producing in China, and conducting R&D in China. Proximity to China is another factor that has strengthened the economic relationship between Korea and China. As long as their economic environments are in harmony and the mutually beneficial economic relationship between the two countries is sustained, this would be a good bet for Korea. However, we are not sure what the net effect of greater engagement with China will be in the future.

Will Korea continue to enjoy opportunity in China? Could there be a "boomerang effect" from China? Could China carve out a portion of the world market and exclude Korea? There are no straightforward answers to these questions, which are part of Korea's conflicting perceptions about China.

Reform Education

Creative and innovative thinking consists of more than merely absorbing existing knowledge. Fostering true creativity will require educational reform at all levels—primary, secondary, and tertiary. An adequate supply of highly educated and trained researchers will be necessary for Korea to make further progress in S&T. As of 2003, the ratio of scientists and engineers to the total higher education degree holders in Korea was significantly higher than in the United States, Japan, and many other industrialized countries. However, the number of scientists and engineers per 10,000 people is lower in Korea than in other advanced countries, mainly because the general ratio of highly educated people to the total population is lower in Korea. Therefore, Korea must continue to support broader access to higher education. In addition, the quality of graduate-level education needs more attention. Compared to that of advanced countries, graduate-level education in Korea is quite underdeveloped, even though it has been improving recently. The Korean Ministry of Education and Human Resource Development has put a great deal of effort into its "BK 21" project to improve graduate education in the 21st century.

Pursue Openness

Using the strategy of openness as a growth engine, China has achieved explosive economic growth and impressive technological progress even though it is still a socialist country with a less sophisticated market systems than some other developing countries. Few countries remain economically isolated since China opened its doors and other former socialist countries have also made the transition to a market economy. However, in the eyes of foreign investors, Korea is still a hostile country for foreign investment. Many foreign business leaders think Korea is relatively isolated from active global networking.

Even with its worldwide penetration of broad-band Internet, Korea has not yet carved out a significant market in the internet or software business. In contrast, India takes over $100 billion in business from global software outsourcing by 185 Fortune 500 companies, according to the UNDP (2001). Both India and China have strong links with Silicon Valley, and the further development of information technology will continue to enhance the ability of multinational corporations to tie together globally distributed laboratories and firms.

Korea is a small country with a limited domestic market and is less attractive to foreign investors than China, Hong Kong, or Singapore. Therefore, Korea must emphasize both exploring opportunities on the world market and bringing in investment and business activities from abroad. Korea needs to pursue a strategy of allowing capital and labor to go abroad to find the best investment and job opportunities while at the same time improving the attractiveness of the country as a place for an increasingly mobile workforce to live.

Future Scenarios

The net effect of the four strategies on Korea's economic prosperity would depend on how the future develops—which, of course, is quite uncertain. Based on the four basic strategies, we analyzed possible future scenarios for Korea's economic performance. Instead of traditional analysis, which uses a few future scenarios that assume a "most likely" future, we looked for alternative strategies that appear to be robust across the full range of uncertainties in the future.

We built a simple model of the Korean economy and introduced four representative strategies, each with a particular focus: (1) "Base"—keeping Korea's current policies, including heavy engagement in the China market and a focus on IT industry; (2) "Openness"—looking to other challenging markets besides China; (3) "R&D"; and (4) "Education."

We then generated 100 scenarios for each strategy, taking advantage of the state of the art in computer technology, and examined how the payoffs to Korea's strategies change over different future situations.

At least in our simple model, the current course for Korean growth, characterized as the "Base" strategy, seems to have the greatest potential for sustained growth under optimal conditions. However, it seems vulnerable to several potential shocks, including a sudden drop in China's growth rate, a greater demand for technological value added, or the narrowing of the technology gap between Korea and China.

On the other hand, the "R&D" strategy seems to be a more robust strategy, providing relatively good results even if China's economic growth slowed down and the demand of technological contents for Korean products were high. In fact, the "R&D" strategy is either optimal or comes within 5 percent of the optimal values in 91 out of our 100 spanning scenarios.

Maintaining a technical advantage over China—or at least keeping the technological gap between Korea and China as wide as possible—could be an insurance policy against stressful times in the future and could maintain the relative attractiveness of Korean products if there is a downturn in China's economic development. And though not specifically modeled in this exercise, it would also give Korea a greater opportunity to explore and develop a presence in more challenging markets.

Our four strategies represent the presumed results of various policies. The names of the strategies merely characterize them by referring to the central element of each. In reality, each strategy is a mixture of varying policy elements. For example, the "R&D" strategy includes a whole range of policy measures to enhance the accumulation of knowledge—such as increasing R&D intensity, reasserting a commitment to basic research and generic technologies, and making institutional innovations to enhance R&D efficiency. In addition, the strategies are not exclusive to each other. The "R&D" strategy by no means disregards the importance of such other fundamentals as educational reform for creativity, openness toward the world, and global networking. Although our four strategies are necessarily simple, exploring them highlights the value of their most important elements and serves as a means to make concrete some of the qualitative issues that are presently being discussed in Korea.

Additional Specifications for the Model of the Korean National Economy

To keep Chapter Six accessible to general readers, that chapter discussed only the most characteristic equations upon which the simple Korean economic model is based. We include the balance of the equations in this appendix. For ease of explanation and for the sake of brevity, we use words instead of symbols in the equations presented below.

Additional Model Equations

Growth of Capital Stock

$$K_t = (1 - \text{Depreciation Rate}) \times K_{t-1} + (1 + \text{Investment Rate}) \times \text{GDP}_{t-1}$$

where K_t is the capital stock at time t and GDP_t is the size of the national economy at time t.

Growth of Labor Force

$$N_t = (1 + \text{Population Growth}) \times (1 + \text{Job Creation Rate}) \times N_{t-1}$$

where N_t is the numbers of workers at time t and the Job Creation Rate is as described in Chapter Six. The value used in the model for effective labor force is

$$L_t = N_t \times \text{Work Days per Year} \times \text{Adjusted Labor Effect} .$$

Growth in Stock of R&D Inputs

$$RD_t = (1 + \text{R\&D Growth Rate}) \times RD_{t-1}$$

where RD_t is the size of the stock of R&D inputs to production at time t. Note that no depreciation rate is assumed for these inputs. On the other hand, no time term symbolizing disembodied technological change has been included in the principal production function equation, Equation (6.3).

Changes in Other Variables

The following variables are entered into the model as inputs representing average annual growth rates across the period being examined:

- Rate of growth in PRC GDP
- Rate of growth in Korean FDI in PRC
- Won/yen rate of appreciation
- Won/U.S. dollar rate of appreciation
- Growth of Korean population.

The related factor associated with each of these rate inputs (e.g., PRC GDP) then increases annually at the rate assigned.

Elasticities of output for capital, labor, and R&D inputs are also present as variable model inputs. For the purpose of the analysis presented in Chapter Six, however, these remain fixed across time periods.

Major National S&T Programs in China: Objectives and Resources

Table B.1 shows the program type, starting year, objectives, and main characteristics of China's major national S&T programs.

Table B.1
Major National S&T Programs in China: Objectives and Resources

Program Type	Program	Starting Year	Objectives	Main Characteristics	Expenditure and/or Budget
Basic research	Key basic science R&D program (973 Program)	1997	To strengthen original and independent innovation capabilities in important areas of basic sciences. To generate new discoveries, theories, and inventions so as to provide scientific foundations for future development.	The 973 Program's specific tasks are to support the implementation of key basic research in important scientific fields such as agriculture, energy resources, information, resources and environment, and population and health; to provide a theoretical basis and scientific foundation for innovation; to foster the development of R&D personnel; and to establish high-level scientific research units.[a]	Exp. (1997–2002): RMB 2.5 billion US $302 million Budget (2004): RMB 0.9 billion (US $109 million)
	NSFC-funded research projects	1986	To support peer-reviewed basic research projects and to foster research talents.	Between 1986 and 2001, the NSFC funded more than 52,000 research projects with an investment of RMB 6.6 billion. More than 60,000 scientists are supported *annually* by NSFC to conduct basic research. In addition, 7,400 young researchers have been given grants from the Young Scientists Fund. NSFC has made important contributions in promoting the progress of Chinese basic research and in nurturing talent.[b]	Exp. (2003): RMB 2.24 billion (US $271 million)[c] Budget (2004): RMB 2.24 billion (US $271 million)

Table B.1—continued

Program Type	Program	Starting Year	Objectives	Main Characteristics	Expenditure and/or Budget
Applied R&D	High-technology R&D program (863 Program)	1986	To enhance China's international competitiveness and overall capability in high-tech R&D by pooling best R&D resources in the nation.	863 Program is China's strategic high-tech R&D program. During the 10th five-year plan period (2001–2005), the civilian area of the program has 19 subject topics from six priority areas: IT, biotechnology and modern agriculture technology, new materials, advanced manufacturing and automation, energy, resources and environment.[d] The civilian R&D areas are under the management of MOST. Other area includes space and laser that have military applications and are managed by the Commission of S&T and Industry for National Defense (COSTIND).	Exp. (1986–2001): RMB5.7 billion (US $689 million) in civilian areas. Budget (2001–2005): RMB 15 billion (US $1.81 billion)
	Key Technology R&D Program	1983	To pool national resources on key and generic technologies that are urgently needed by industrial upgrading and social sustainable development.	The focus of the program during the 10th five-year plan period (2001–2005) is in four priority areas: (1) technologies that have a significant role in advancing agriculture; (2) industrial upgrading technologies (e.g., informatization of traditional manufacturing industries, automation); (3) key technologies in population, resources, and the environment as well as national security (e.g., major disaster forecast and prevention, birth control, and key technology standards); (4) nurturing competent R&D workforce and establishing a cluster of technology innovation bases of international standing.[e]	Exp. (1996–2000): RMB 22.9 billion of which treasury appropriation was RMB 5.3 billion. Budget (2001–2005): n/a but treasury appropriation is reported to be RMB 5 billion (US $604 million)

Table B.1—continued

Program Type	Program	Starting Year	Objectives	Main Characteristics	Expenditure and/or Budget
Industrialization	Torch Program	1988	To accelerate the industrialization of high technology, promote commercialization of R&D results, foster high-tech startups.	53 "High-tech Industry Development Zones" (HTIDZs) were established throughout China by the end of 2003, accommodating 33,000 firms and 3.95 million employees. HTIDZs are a major force in China's high-tech exports (US $51 billion in 2003). Various technology incubators and Productivity Promotion Centers (PPCs) were also set up under Torch to facilitate technology transfer, nurture high-tech-based companies and entrepreneurs, and provide training.	Sources of funds are mainly public with support of start-up funds from the PRC Government Exp./budget not clear
	Spark Program	1986	To support appropriate technology transfer to rural area to foster township enterprise development.	Government funding for the program has been insignificant (e.g., 2.2% of total funding in 2000). Enterprises' own capital and bank loans were the main sources of the capital for the projects, accounting for 81% and 16.8% of total. By the end of 2000, there was a cumulative total of 111,851 Spark projects over various parts of China.	Total investment (1986–2000):f RMB 310 billion (US $37.5 billion) Budget 2004: n/a
	The Innovation Fund for Small Technology Based Firms	1999	To support the start-up of firms based on new and high technologies.	Fund support was said to be instrumental for the start-up of technology-based ventures, as the award could help to pull in other resources such as local government funding, financing from banks, and financial institutions etc.9	Exp. (1999–2003): RMB 2.85 billion (US $344 million)h Budget (2004): unkown

Table B.1—continued

Program Type	Program	Starting Year	Objectives	Main Characteristics	Expenditure and/or Budget
Infra-structure	National Key Laboratories (NKLs) Program	1984	To support and improve selected laboratories at universities and research institutes. NKLs are open to researchers nationwide.	As of September 2004, there were 159 NKLs in China. Each laboratory is specialized in a field and is equipped with modern scientific equipments and apparatus. The NKLs have played an important role in the cultivation of R&D talents in China and have enhanced China's R&D capabilities.	Exp. (2002): RMB 2.0 billion[i] (US$242 million)
					Budget 2004: n/a
	National Engineering Centers (NECs)		To support technology transfer and assimilation, commercialization of R&D results, and industrialization.	NECs are designed to be centers for technology exchange as well as engineering technology contractors; most operate as enterprises (i.e., profit-seeking).	Exp.: n/a
				There were 128 NECs by the end of 2003. During the 10th five-year plan period (2001–2005), 50 more NECs will be built.	Income (2003): RMB 7.97 billion (US $963 million)

SOURCE: Huang et al. (2004) and other sources identified in the notes.

a "Profile of 973 Program," from official 973 Program Web site, online at www.973.gov.cn/English/Index.aspx, accessed 12 October 2004.

b "Past achievements of NSFC," online at www.nsfc.org.cn/e_nsfc/desktop/zn/cg/qianyan.htm, accessed 10 September 2004.

c "NSFC Annual Report 2003" (in Chinese), online at www.nsfc.org.cn/nsfc/cen/nndbg/2003ndbg/index.htm, accessed 10 October 2004.

d "Brief introduction to the 863 Program during the 10th five-year plan," from official 863 Program Web site, www.863.org.cn/863_105/863brief/105_863/20040508286.html, accessed 12 October 2004

Table B.1—continued

e "Key technology R&D program under the 10th five-year plan" (in Chinese), available from CMOST, www.gongguan.most.gov.cn/intro105.htm, accessed 12 October 2004.

f "Spark Program annual report 2000," online at www.cnsp.org.cn/ndbg/ndbg2000.htm, (in Chinese), accessed 10 September 2004.

g Ma Songde, Vice Minister of MOST, "Making use of the pulling effects of Innovation Fund to promote the development of Small Technology Based Firms," 21 March 2003, online at www.cas.ac.cn/html/Dir/2003/03/21/7045.htm, accessed 20 September 2004.

h "Transformation of R&D institutions—Minister Xu on China's S&T reform and development," China.org, 20 February 2003, online at www.china.org.cn/chinese/2003/Feb/279880.htm, accessed 20 September 2004.

i "Statistical report of National Key Laboratories—2002," online at www.chinalab.gov.cn/stat/select0819.asp?year=2002, (in Chinese), accessed 12 October 2004.

References

Archibugi, D., and A. Coco, "The Measurement of International Technological Capabilities: A Comparison of Different Approaches and Methodologies," Italian National Research Council, Rome, 2003.

_____, "A New Indicator of Technological Capabilities for Developed and Developing Countries (ArCo)," SPRU Electronic Working Paper Series, #111, January 2004.

Arnold, W., "The Japanese Automobile Industry in China," Japan Policy Research Institute Working Paper No. 95, November 2003, online at www.jpri.org/publications/workingpapers/wp95.html, accessed 15 September 2004.

Bank of Korea, "World Semiconductor Market Overview and Future Prospects," *Overseas Economic Information* 2003-81, 2003.

Berthoin A., and W. Jin, "Organizational Learning in China: The Role of Returners," Discussion Paper SP III 2003-103, Wissenschaftszentrum Berlin für Sozialforschung (2003), online at skylla.wz-berlin.de/pdf/2003/iii03-103.pdf, accessed 14 September 2004.

Bureau of Economic Analysis, Gross-Domestic-Product-(GDP)-by-Industry Data (2002), online at www.bea.gov/bea/dn2/gdpbyind_data.htm.

Chase, Michael S., K. L. Pollpeter, and J. C. Mulvenon, *Shanghaied? The Economic and Political Implications of the Flow of Information Technology and Investment Across the Taiwan Strait,* RAND Corporation, Santa Monica, Calif., TR-133-RC, 2004.

Chen, C., L. Chung, and Y. Zhang, "The Role of Foreign Direct Investment in China's Post-1978 Economic Development," *World Development* 23(4), 1995, 691–703.

Chen, Y. C., "Restructuring the Shanghai Innovation System: The Role of Multinational Corporations' R&D Centers in Shanghai," presented at The First ASIANLICS International Conference: Innovation Systems and Clusters in Asia—Challenges and Regional Integration, Bangkok, Thailand, 1–2 April 2004.

Chen Z., "Making S&T Evaluation the Tools for Government Decision-Making: Practice in China," Proceedings of the APEC Symposium on the Evaluation of S&T Programs Among APEC Member Economies, 2–4 December 1998, Wellington, New Zealand, online at National Center for S&T Evaluation (NCSTE), online at www.apecevalu. org/content/PRChina.htm, accessed 5 September 2004.

Cheong, Y. R., *Chinese Business Networks and Their Implication for South Korea,* Institute of International Economics, Washington, D.C., 2003.

Cheung K., and P. Lin, "Spillover Effects of FDI on Innovation in China: Evidence from the Provincial Data," *China Economic Review* 15, 2004, 25–44.

China Ministry of Education (CMOE), *Education Statistical Report 2002,* Vol. 26, 27 February 2003.

China Ministry of Science and Technology (CMOST) (2000), "Tenth Five Year High-Tech Development Plan," online at gh.most.gov. cn/zcq/ShowContent.jsp?db=KJGHSWZDZXGH&id=7 (in Chinese).

_____ (2003a), *China Technology Foresight 2003 Report* (in Chinese), Scientific and Technical Documents Publishing House, Ministry of Science and Technology, Beijing, 2003a.

_____ (2003b), *China S&T Statistics Data Book 2003* (in Chinese), online at www.sts.org.cn/sjkl/kjtjdt/data2003/cstsm03.htm, accessed 25 August 2004.

_____ (2003c), *China S&T Indicators 2002* (The S&T Yellow Book), in both Chinese and English. Can be ordered at www.most.gov.cn.

_____ (2004), "21 National Key Technologies Towards the 21st Century—The National Key Technologies Selection Report No. 1" (in Chinese), Technology Foresight and National Key Technology Selection Group, online at www.foresight.org.cn/dybg/2004guanjianjishu21.htm, accessed 20 August 2004.

China Science and Technology Statistical Year Book 2003. Statistical Publishers, Beijing, 2003.

China Statistical Year Book, 1996, 2001, 2002, and 2003 editions, Statistical Publishers, Beijing.

Chinese Academy of Sciences (CAS), *Science Development Report 2002,* online at www.cas.cn/html/Books/O6121/b1/2003/index.htm#6.

_____, "Construction of China's National Innovation System," Chinese Academy of Sciences, 2003, online at english.cas.ac.cn/eng2003/news/detailnewsb.asp?InfoNo=20966.

Cohen, D., and M. Soto, "Growth and Human Capital: Good Data, Good Results," OECD Development Center Technical Papers No. 179, Paris, September 2001.

Dahlman, C. J., and J-E Aubert, "China and the Knowledge Economy: Seizing the 21st Century," World Bank, Washington, D.C., 2001, online at www-wds.worldbank.org/servlet/WDS_IBank_Servlet?pcont=details&eid=000094946_01102704134061.

Desai, M., et al., "How Well Are People Participating in the Benefits of Technological Progress? Technological Achievement Index (TAI)," Background Paper for UNDP, United Nations, New York, 2001.

Economist Intelligence Unit, "Scattering the Seeds of Invention: The Globalisation of Research and Development," September 2004, online at www.eiu.com/GlobalisationOfRandD, accessed 23 December 2004.

Fan, E. X, "Technological Spillovers from Foreign Direct Investment—A Survey," Economic and Research Development (ERD) Working Paper No. 33, Asia Development Bank, 2002, online at www.adb.org/Documents/ERD/Working_Papers/wp033.pdf, accessed 25 September 2004.

Ferguson, R. W., and W. L. Wascher, Distinguished Lecture on Economics in Government: "Lessons from Past Productivity Booms," *Journal of Economic Perspectives* 18(2), 2004, 3–28.

"Formidable Chinese Technology: Technological Capability of China Will Surpass That of Korea in 10 Years," *Chosun Ilbo,* 30

July 2004, online at www.chosun.com/w21data/html/new/200407/200407300454.html.

Freeman, C., *Technology and Economic Performance: Lessons from Japan,* Pinter, London, 1987.

Hsiung, Deh-I, "An Evaluation of China's Science & Technology System and its Impact on the Research Community", A Special Report for the Environment, Science & Technology Section, U.S. Embassy, Beijing, Summer 2002, online at www.usembassy-china.org.cn/sandt/S&T-Report.doc, accessed 29 August 2004.

Hu, Albert, and Gary Jefferson, "FDI Impact and Spillover: Evidence from China's Electronic and Textile Industries." *World Economy* 25(8), August 2002, 1063.

Hu, Albert, Gary H. Jefferson, and Qian Jinchang, "R&D and Technology Transfer in Chinese Industry," *Review of Economics and Statistics,* forthcoming.

Huang, C. C., et al., "Organization, Program, and Structure: An Analysis of the Chinese Innovation Policy Framework," forthcoming in *R&D Management,* Special Edition: "Managing R&D in China," 2004.

International Development Research Centre (IDRC), "A Decade of Reform—Science and Technology Policy in China," IDRC and the State Science and Technology Commission (People's Republic of China), 1997, online at web.idrc.ca/en/ev-9360-201-1-DO_TOPIC.html, accessed 4 January 2005.

International Monetary Fund (IMF), *International Financial Statistics Yearbook 2004,* Washington, D.C., 2004.

Kelly, C., et al., *High-Technology Manufacturing and U.S. Competitiveness,* RAND Corporation, Santa Monica, Calif., TR-136-OSTP, 2004.

Korea Development Bank (KBD), "Technological Competitiveness Analysis of Major Industries in Korea, China, and Japan," KDB Technology Report No. 31, Seoul, 2004.

Korea Development Institute (KDI), *Comprehensive Study on Industrial Competitiveness of Korea,* Vol. 1–2, Seoul, 2003.

Korea Institute of Science and Technology Evaluation and Planning (KISTEP 2004a), *Overview of the Government R&D Budget in 2004,* Seoul.

_____ (KISTEP 2004b), *Technology Level Evaluation*, Seoul, 2004.

Korea International Trade Association (KITA), *Republic of Korea: 207 Indicators of Economy, Trade, and Society*, Seoul, 2004.

Korea Ministry of Education and Human Resource Development (KMEHRD), *2004 Education Statistical Yearbook*, Seoul, 2004.

Korea Ministry of Science and Technology (KMOST), *Overview of Academic Paper Publication in Engineering: Analysis of Compendex of EI, 2001*. www.most.go.kr/.

_____, "News release: Analysis of Science Citation Index (SCI) of 2003," Seoul, 2004.

_____, *2003 Science and Technology Research Activity Report*, Seoul, 2004.

Korean Industrial Technology Association, *Major Indicators of Industrial Technology*, 2003/2004 Edition, Seoul, 2004.

Kranhold, K., "China's Price for Market Entry: Give Us Your Technology, Too," *Wall Street Journal*, 26 February 2004, p. 1.

Lall, S., "Competitiveness Indices and Developing Countries: An Economic Evaluation of the Global Competitiveness Report," *World Development* 29(9), 2001, 1501–1525.

Lall, S., and M. Albaladejo, "Indicators of the Relative Importance of IPTs in Developing Countries," UNCTAD, Geneva, 2001, online at www.ictsd.org/unctad-ictsd/.

Lempert, R., S. Popper, and S. Bankes, *Shaping the Next One Hundred Years: New Methods for Quantitative Long-Term Policy Analysis*, RAND Corporation, Santa Monica, Calif., MG-1626-OSTP, 2003.

Liu, C., and J. Yang, "A Comparative Analysis of Technology Innovation and Diffusion Systems, and Industrial Innovation Between Taiwan And Mainland China," *International Journal of Innovation Management* 7(4), December 2003.

Liu, H., and Y. Jiang, "Technology Transfer from Higher Education Institutions to Industry in China: Nature and Implications," *Technovation* 21, 2001, 175–188.

Liu, X., and S. White, "Comparing Innovation Systems: A Framework and Application to China's Transitional Context," *Research Policy* 30, 2001, 1091–1114.

Metcalfe, S., "The Economic Foundations of Technology Policy: Equilibrium and Evolutionary Perspectives," in P. Stoneman (ed.), *Handbook of the Economics of Innovation and Technological Change,* Blackwell Publishers, Oxford (UK)/Cambridge (U.S.), 1995.

Motohashi, Kazuyuki, "Fall of Japanese Competitiveness in 1990s? Assessment of Structural Factors Behind Economic Growth Slowdown and Policy Initiatives," KDI 33rd Anniversary Conference on Industrial Dynamism and Competitiveness in the East Asian Economies, 22–23 April 2004.

Mowery, D., and R. Nelson, *Sources of Industrial Leadership: Studies of Seven Industries,* Cambridge University Press, New York, 1999.

Moyer, B., et al., "Improved Annual Industry Accounts for 1998–2003: Integrated Annual Input-Output Accounts and Gross-Domestic-Product-by-Industry Accounts," *Survey of Current Business,* Bureau of Economic Analysis, Washington, D.C., June 2004.

National Institute of Science and Technology Policy (NISTP), "The Seventh Technology Foresight—Future Technology in Japan Toward the Year 2030," NISTEP Report No. 71, Ministry of Education, Culture, Sports, Science and Technology of Japan, July 2001, online at www.nistep.go.jp/index-e.html, accessed 28 August 2004.

National Science Foundations (NSF), *Science and Engineering Indicators,* National Science Board, Washington, D.C., 2004.

Ng, Francis, and Alexander Yeats, "Production Sharing in East Asia: Who Does What for Whom, and Why?" Policy Research Working Paper Series 2197, World Bank, Washington, D.C., 1999.

Organization for Economic Cooperation and Development (OECD) (1997), *National Innovation Systems,* Paris, 1997.

_____ (1999a), *Managing National Innovation Systems,* Paris, 1999.

_____ (1999b), *Strategic Business Services,* Paris, 1999.

_____ (2001), *Basic Science and Technology Statistics,* Paris, 2001.

_____ (2002a), "Science And Technology in China: Trends and Policy Challenges," *OECD Science, Technology and Industry Outlook,* Paris, 2002.

_____ (2002b), *China in the World Economy,* Paris, 2002.

_____ (2004), *Main Science and Technology Indicators,* Paris, May 2004.

_____, *STIC Scoreboard,* Paris, (various years).

Park, R., and H. Yang, "Controversy over Manufacturing Hollow Out," *LG Economic Weekly,* LG Economic Research Institute (LGERI), 3 March 2004.

Popper, Steven W., et al., *New Forces at Work: Industry Views Critical Technologies,* RAND Corporation, Santa Monica, Calif., MR-1008-1-OSTP, 1998.

Porter, A. L., et al., "Measuring National 'Emerging Technology' Capabilities," *Science and Public Policy* 29(3), June 2002.

Porter, M. E., *The Competitive Advantage of Nations,* The Free Press, New York, 1990.

Saxenian, AnnaLee, "Brain Circulation and Capitalist Dynamics: The Silicon Valley-Hsinchu-Shanghai Triangle," The Center for Economy and Society, Cornell University, Department of Sociology, CSES Working Papers Series Paper No. 8, August 2003, online at www.economyandsociety.org/publications/wp8.pdf, accessed 10 Sept 2004.

Seong, Somi, "Korea's Industrial Development, Globalization, and Prospects for Regional and Global Integration," KDI working paper 2001-03, Korea Development Institute, Seoul, 2003.

Shin, T., *Contribution of R&D Investment to Economic Growth,* Korea Science and Technology Policy Institute (STEPI), Seoul, 2004.

Shin, T., et al., "Study on Hollowing-out of Manufacturing: Impacts of Foreign Direct Investment and Trade Balance on Manufacturing," Policy Study 2003-04, STEPI, Seoul, Korea, 2003.

Suttmeier, R. P., and C. Cao, "China Faces the New Industrial Revolution: Achievement and Uncertainty in the Search for Research and Innovation Strategies," *Asian Perspective* 23(3), 26 November 1999.

Suttmeier, R. P., and X. Yao, "China's Post-WTO Technology Policy: Standards, Software, and the Changing Nature of Techno-Nationalism," Special Report of the National Bureau of Asian Research, No. 7, May 2004.

Tan, A. A., "Product Cycle Theory and Telecommunication Industry: Foreign Direct Investment, Government Policy, and Indigenous Manufacturing in China," *Telecommunications Policy,* 26, 2002, 17-30.

Technology Review and CHI Research, *The TR Patent Scorecard 2004,* 2004.

Tseng, Wanda S., and Harm H. Zebregs, "Foreign Direct Investment in China: Some Lessons for Other Countries," International Monetary Fund, Washington, D.C., Policy Discussion Paper No. 02/3, 2002.

Tung, C-Y, "Foreign Direct Investment in China and Its Contribution to China's Economic Development," China Economic Analysis Working Papers No. 2, August 2003, online at cea.future-china.org.tw/pdf/Working%20papers/200308-2WPE.pdf, accessed 4 October 2004.

United Nations Conference on Trade and Development (UNCTAD), "Foreign Direct Investment Data," online at www.unctad.org/Templates/Page.asp?intItemID=1923&lang=1, accessed 4 January 2005.

_____, "China: An Emerging FDI Outward Investor," UNCTAD eBrief, 4 December 2003, online at www.unctad.org/Templates/Webflyer.asp?docID=4295&intItemID=2068&lang=1.

United Nations Development Programme (UNDP), *Human Development Report 2001: Making New Technologies Work for Human Development,* Oxford University Press, New York, 2001.

United Nations Educational, Scientific and Cultural Organization (UNESCO), *World Education Indicators,* Paris, 2002.

United Nations Industrial Development Organization (UNIDO), *Industrial Development Report 2002–2003: Competing Through Innovation and Learning,* Vienna, 2002.

United States Patent and Trademark Office (USPTO), Registered Patent Database, Washington, D.C., 2002, www.uspto.org.

_____, Information Products Division, Technology Assessment and Forecast Branch, special tabulations, November 2002.

_____, Information Products Division, Technology Assessment and Forecast Branch, special tabulations, 2003.

Wagner, Caroline S., et al., *Science & Technology Collaboration: Building Capacity in Developing Countries,* MR-1357-WB, RAND Corporation, Santa Monica, Calif., 2000.

Wagner, Caroline S., Edwin Horlings, and Arindam Dutta, "A Science and Technology Capacity Index: Input for Decision Making," *International Journal of Technology and Globalization* (forthcoming 2005).

Walsh, K., "Foreign High-Tech R&D in China: Risks, Rewards, and Implications for US-China Relations," The Henry L. Stimson Center, 2003, online at www.stimson.org/pubs.cfm?ID=82, accessed 19 August 2004.

Wang, X., and X. Li, The Contribution of FDI to China's Industrial Growth and Technological Progress, Chinese Academy of Social Sciences, online at www.usc.cuhk.edu.hk/wk_wzdetails.asp?id=2494 (in Chinese), accessed 4 October 2004.

World Bank, World Development Indicators, Washington, D.C., 2003.

World Economic Forum (WEF), Global Competitiveness Report 2001–2002, Oxford University Press, New York, 2002.

Yang, Pyung-sup, Long Term Prospects of Korea's Trade with China, Korea Trade Research Institute (KITA), 2004.

Yang, Q-Q, et al., "Technology Foresight and Critical Technology Selection in China," International Journal of Foresight and Innovation Policy 1(1/2), 2004, 168–180.

Young, S., and P. Lan, "Technology Transfer to China Through Foreign Direct Investment," Regional Studies, 31(7), 1997, 669–679.

Zhang, J., and Y. Ouyang, "Foreign Direct Investment's Spillover Effects—The Case of Guangdong Province," China Economics Quarterly 2(3), April 2003 (in Chinese with English abstract), online at www.ccer.edu.cn/download/ceq/2.3/020309.pdf, accessed 4 January 2005.

Zhang, W., and R. Taylor, "EU Technology Transfer to China: The Automotive Industry as a Case Study," Journal of the Asia Pacific Economy, 2001 6(2), 261–274.

Zhu Rongji, "Report on the Work of the Government to the First Session of the 10th National People's Congress by Premier Zhu Rongji," 5 March 2003, online at http://english.pladaily.com.cn/special/e-10th/, accessed 25 August 2004.